Jeffrey Ames Kay

Theological Aesthetics

The Role of Aesthetics in the Theological Method
of Hans Urs von Balthasar

European University Papers

Europäische Hochschulschriften
Publications Universitaires Européennes

Series XXIII

Theology

Reihe XXIII   Série XXIII

Theologie
Théologie

Vol./Bd. 60

Jeffrey Ames Kay

Theological Aesthetics

The Role of Aesthetics in the Theological Method
of Hans Urs von Balthasar

Herbert Lang Bern
Peter Lang Frankfurt/M.
1975

Jeffrey Ames Kay

Theological Aesthetics

The Role of Aesthetics in the Theological Method
of Hans Urs von Balthasar

Herbert Lang Bern
Peter Lang Frankfurt/M.
1975

ISBN 3 261 01893 3
©
Herbert Lang&Co. Ltd., Bern (Switzerland)
Peter Lang Ltd., Frankfurt/M. (West-Germany)
1975. All rights reserved.

Printed by fotokop wilhelm weihert KG, Darmstadt

TABLE OF CONTENTS

PART II

THE SPLENDOR OF CHRIST IN THEOLOGICAL METHOD

INTRODUCTION

Any theological method that fails to recognize the central role of aesthetics is doomed to be dull and unconvincing. This must be so if the object of theology is Christ, the personified love-relation between God and man. If the task of theology is to present the truth of that relation by assisting it to reveal its own truth, the theologian's prime task is to lead others to "see" the balance, proportion and tension within the form of Christ and then to be enraptured by its splendor. This selfless enrapturing vision of the splendor of Christ's form is the basic moment of self-verification in Christian theology. The satisfaction of human needs and expectations as a criterion of verification must be clearly subordinated to it. Verification occurs when a viewer is so fascinated that he has neither time nor desire to think about himself and what benefits he can derive from such beauty. Theology, therefore, must be concerned much less with showing man that Christ offers him what he wants and much more concerned with showing man that he cannot help but worship the splendor of what he sees.

For this reason Hans Urs von Balthasar sees the role of aesthetics in theological method as the major question dividing much Protestant theology from much Catholic theology. The Lutheran concentration on the "beneficia Christi" as the proper object of theology and the Kantian insistence that God can be known only by practical reason have led many theologians to ignore the importance of aesthetics in theology. Ritschl, Harnack and Bultmann within Protestantism and Marechal, Rahner, Welte and Coreth within Catholicism stand profoundly under the influence of Kant and thus place little emphasis on the contemplation of form and on rapture by its beauty. Balthasar's study entitled Herrlichkeit, Eine Theologische Aesthetik (Splendor, A Theological Aesthetics) was written to counteract this tendency and was directed primarily against the influence of Bultmann. Through his emphasis on the vision of form he hoped to guide Protestant theology out of and Catholic theology away from the continual vacillation between a blind neo-orthodoxy and an all-seeing liberalism. Preserving the distance of contemplation and a reverence for form prevents the reduction of man to God (theopanism) in neo-orthodoxy and an all-seeing of God to man (pantheism) in liberalism. He counteracts their mutual tendency toward monism by demonstrating the ability of the finite to reveal the infinite and by describing the beauty of that revelation. By thus establishing the unsurpassable dignity of both form and its beauty, he grounds the unsurpassable dignity of human finitude and human evidence. He prevents human evidence from either being ultimately consumed by divine evidence or ultimately consuming divine evidence. God speaks as man but neither does God become identical with man nor man with God.

Personally Balthasar is a man of great reserve and of fierce commitment to his work and his theological position. These qualities have caused him to find himself in the prophetic role during much of his life and, therefore, often out of his time. Before the Second Vatican Council he was in considerable conflict with conservative powers within the Roman Church and since Vatican II he has been attacking many of the more liberal theological currents within Christianity. His personal intensity manifests itself most clearly in the high degree of spiritual development that he expects from all Christians.

He was born in 1905 in Luzern, Switzerland, to an aristocratic and highly musical family. As a youth he was a passionate and even voracious student and well on his way towards a literary and musical career. After obtaining a doctorate in German literature, he entered the Society of Jesus. His theological studies in Lyons brought him into contact with the French theological renaissance (la nouvelle theologie) that prepared the way for Vatican II. Its mentor was Henri de Lubac whom Balthasar reveres as the greatest man of the spirit he has ever known. De Lubac opened up to him the riches of patristic theology which have remained the most fruitful seedbed of his own theology.

After completing his theological studies he worked on the Jesuit quarterly Stimmen der Zeit in Munich and came under the influence of Eric Przywara and later of Karl Barth. Both men intensified the strong Christocentric orientation of his theology that has led him in all of his writings to dwell primarily on Christ as unexpectable, unsurpassable and incomprehensible. His recent volumes on theological aesthetics are the culmination of many writings that portray Christ as infinitely more that what man wants and needs him to be. This "more" must be seen clearly in order to present a credible Christian theology. The Christian must see the useless, profitless, unpredictable character of God's love in order to understand. This will overburden him psychologically and destroy all the harmony of a closed humanism. In this mutual helplessness of the Christian and the crucified Christ lies the Christian's transparency to Christ's splendor.

Balthasar sees this transparency increasing the more intensely a Christian lives the evangelical counsels. He regards the "secular institute" as a significant way of living the counsels today and has devoted much of his time since 1940 to the development of such an institute in Basel.

Although it was in order to found this institute that he left the Jesuits he sees the institute as the contemporary continuation of what Ignatius wanted in his own time. It is composed of a small group of laymen living the evangelical counsels in a shared life yet each pursuing his chosen secular profession. The impetus to found the institute came in large part from Adrienne von Speyr, a visionary and mystic, with whom Balthasar was bound in a profound friendship until her death in 1967. She dictated to him commentaries on most of the books of the Old and New Testaments which he has published in his own publishing house, Johannes Verlag. He writes that his and her writings cannot be sundered psychologically or philologically, that they are two halves of a whole and share a common midpoint.

His own writings have developed his central theme in an overwhelming variety of approaches. There seems to be few sources in Western literature, philosophy and theology that are not readily at his disposal in the orchestration of his theme. Important among those sources are the Greek Tragedians, pre-Judaic Old Testament writings, the Evangelist John, Irenaeus, Augustine, Thomas, Nicholas of Cues, Ignatius of Loyola and Goethe. All of them share his concern with the perception of form.

His two volumes on the theology of history: Theologie der Geschichte (Eng.

trans. The Theology of History) (A27) and Das Ganze im Fragment (Eng. trans.
Theological Anthropology) (A33)(1) present Christ as the norm and fulfillment of
history. The way in which Christ judges and saves all history is further developed
in his volume of collected essays, Verbum Caro (Eng. trans. Essays in Theology)
(A28). These essays begin a discussion with Karl Barth who shares this concern
with the uniqueness and universality of Christ. The discussion is continued in Karl
Barth (Eng. trans. Karl Barth) (A14) through a comparison of Barth's dialectical
yet universalistic thought with the new understanding of nature and grace being
developed in Catholicism under de Lubac's inspiration.

With these works establishing the objective mid-point, Balthasar devotes
numerous books and articles to the subjective mid-point: to the life of the Church
and of the "saints" within the Church. Sponsa Verbi (Eng. trans. Church and World)
(A29); Das Betrachtende Gebet (Eng. trans. Prayer) (A21); Therese von Lisieux
(A12); Elisabeth von Dijon (A16, B62); Bernanos (A20); Reinhold Schneider (A18);
Wer ist ein Christ (Eng. trans. Who is a Christian) (A37); Glaubhaft ist nur Liebe
(Eng. trans. Love Alone) (A34), and Pneuma und Institution (A54) represent the
most important ecclesiological writings.

A desire to present in a unified way the incomprehensible mid-point of
Christianity as it has existed throughout history led to the idea of writing a theological aesthetics, dramatics and logic. The theological aesthetics has been completed
in five volumes and work has begun on the dramatics. Volume one of the aesthetics
is entitled Schau der Gestalt, seeing the form, (A30) and presents a fundamental
theology from the aesthetic viewpoint. The two parts treat the objective and subjective
evidence for Christianity showing that only selfless love can perceive the self-verify-
ing splendor of Christ's form. Volume two Faecher der Stile, types of styles, (A32)
studies twelve important theologians and poets in an attempt to show the role of divine splendor in various styles of theology. The twelve are composed of four great
theologians of patristic and early medieval theology; Dante, a poet; John of the
Cross, a mystic; Pascal, a thinker; two critics of German idealism, Hamann and
Soloviev; the English Jesuit poet Hopkins; and the French social critic, poet and
dramatist, Charles Peguy. Volume three, Im Raum der Metaphysik, in the realm
of metaphysics, (A36) attempts to show how deeply Christian thought sinks itself
into the thought of humanity. It studies philosophers and poets from Homer to Heidegger for their understanding of transcendent beauty. Taking up Heidegger's attack
on the forgetfulness of Being in contemporary philosophy he calls upon Christian
thinkers to go beyond Heidegger's view of Being to a vision of Absolute Being and
its splendor. The forth and fifth volumes (A41, A46) trace the increasingly intimate presence of divine splendor in the history of Israel and the apostolic church.

---

(1) References with a letter and numbers within parentheses are to the writings of
Balthasar as catalogued by Berthe Widmer in the published bibliography, Rechenschaft, Einsiedeln 1965.

It is extremely important to realize that the aesthetics puts primary emphasis on light, image and vision, leaving decision and action for the dramatics and thought for the logic. Action and thought play an essential role in aesthetics but one cannot expect them to be adequately discussed in Herrlichkeit. After centuries of reducing theology to ethics and logic, however, this extensive treatment of aesthetics is desperately needed. This is especially true in American in a time like our own when beauty, solitude, meditation and creativity are being gradually returned to their medieval position of primacy.

Although Balthasar's work is often considered outdated and dismissed as neo-Platonic, such a mind as Karl Rahner's realizes that it is a theology that few people today are yet ready to understand. "Much more of the seed that he (Balthasar) has strewn in the field of the Church will sprout than what we see now." "Perhaps the effectiveness of such a theology inevitably takes longer than our impatience is ready to tolerate."(2)

Throughout my attempt here to introduce the reader to Balthasar's aesthetics, I have kept the Protestant reader especially in mind. As Balthasar has stated (A44 32), aesthetics allows the deepest understanding of Luther's concern in his doctrine of justification. Its new categories free Lutheran theology of its reliance on in-appropriate juridical categories. That Balthasar does stand close to Luther's deep-est intentions, I will try to show by pointing out the similarity between Balthasar's theological method and that of the most renowned contemporary interpreter of Luther, Gerhard Ebeling. Uniting them both philosophically is their sharing in Heidegger's abhorrence of the forgetfulness of Being. Theologically they share a concern to make the Jesus of history visible and thereby bring out the objective character of revelation (cf. below pp. 47ff   ). Ebeling's emphasis on the word-event and on the situation parallels Balthasar's concern with form. What divides them is Ebeling's strong emphasis on the fulfillment of need as the principle of ver-ification (cf. below pp. 44f). Except for this disagreement there are numerous important points of agreement which I will point out simply by citing an Ebeling text when discussing a point in Balthasar's theology.

If the proximity of Ebeling and Balthasar can lead Protestant theology closer to an appreciation of the contemplation of forms and lead Catholic theology closer to a Christocentrism, it will be a significant step towards the assimilation of Protestant and Catholic theological methods.

Finally my thanks to Dr. von Balthasar for our numerous discussions, his comments on the manuscript, and his continued encouragement. My very special thanks to my wife Josy for the financial and emotional support that made the book possible.

---

(2) Rahner, Karl, "Hans Urs von Balthasar," in Civitas 1965, p. 604.

PART I

THE SPLENDOR OF BEING IN PHILOSOPHICAL METHOD

The first chapter of Part I will treat the contemplative act of wonder before the appearance of limitless Being in limited forms. The following shorter chapters will discuss three spiritualities, eros, action and receptivity, that are implied in contemplative wonder. An over-emphasis on any one of these approaches will inevitably lead to an activism or passivism that eliminates the basic tension between theory and practice required to maintain wonder. In activism the knower reduces reality to voiceless, lifeless, formless matter that evokes no wonder and in passivism reality reduces the knower to the very unwondrous function of the movie camera. In both cases love and therefore beauty are destroyed.

Chapter One

CONTEMPLATION

The Heart

Since wonder begins and ends with the contemplation of form, we must start by asking what it means to perceive a form. The central human organ that perceives form Balthasar designates in good scriptural, patristic and romantic tradition as the heart. Because the heart integrates the intellect, will, emotions and senses, it unites the body and the mind which is fundamental to any form of aesthetics. (A32 202, 425, 857, A36 933) Feeling is the common activity into which the heart integrates and unifies all man's undertakings. As the activity of the heart feeling is not to be regarded with Schleiermacher as a separate faculty along side of the intellect and the will nor as in any way a subhuman faculty. It is the integration of all human faculties and, therefore, eminently human. (A30 234ff)

As the microcosmic culmination of macrocosmic evolution the feeling of man's heart gathers together the activities of the entire cosmos. It actualizes the interpenetration of matter and spirit and it portays the in-born tenderness of the spirit for the body. Through the heart the spirit is able to express itself in the body and thus transform the body into spirit and the spirit into body. (A6 34ff, A33 250) This delicate polarity between body and spirit that the heart effects in feeling prevents both the body and its instincts from dominating the spirit and the spirit from dominating the body.

By rooting the senses in itself the heart makes all sensual activities into acts of the whole man. The senses are man's opened heart. The eye, for instance, is the openness of the whole man to reality insofar as it is form and light. This integration of the mind's vision with the eye's vision is effected not only by their

1

common agent, the heart, but also by their common object, Being. (A30 367-93)

Essence and Existence

The heart perceives Being only in finite, sensible forms so that its first task is to gather sense impressions into unified images. From the image it abstracts an essence that is composed of both a unique changing form (morphe, entelechia) incapable of conceptualization and a universal, necessary, unchanging form (eidos, idea) capable of conceptualization. (A10 132f, 167ff) The concept, therefore, is merely a guess at only one aspect of the image and thus appears greatly impoverished and merely accidental in comparison to the richness of the total image. (A36 380, 569, A10 144, C25 187) Since the conceptualized eidos and the changing morphe never appear separately, the mind must continually move back and forth between the two in an attempt to broaden its concept. This movement constitutes reason's struggle to understand by gathering together (intel-ligence) in one view as many varying morphe as possible within the fixed universal eidos. The ever-changing morphe forces the knower to recognize the immersion of the essence in time. As the prime structure of existence, time forces him in turn to see the difference between essence and existence. When the morphe has revealed how the essence is caught up in the river of time, the essence is seen to be so thoroughly intermeshed with limitless existence that it could never be fully grasped by any one subject at any one time. (A10 166ff) Because the subject in attempting to grasp the essence is at the mercy of the coming and going of the morphe, it too is caught up in the river of history and can know the essences only from moment to moment, from constantly changing perspectives. (A10 170ff) Although the subject is capable of abstracting a concept of the eidos from this flux, it would be absurd for it to absolutize the concept. The conceptualized eidos or essence must constantly be seen anew in its ever-changing existence. The subject must share with other subjects throughout history their new, peculiar perspectives. (A10 149ff, 191f; A30 20; A31 303)

Form

To see this difference between essence and existence is to see existence taking its own measure and positing itself as a form. "Form is a totality of parts and elements that is conceived as limited and standing in itself yet requiring for its preservation not only an environment but ultimately the whole of Being. The finite form is a contracted presentation of infinite Being. By gathering together, unifying and ruling its parts it enables them to transcend towards the infinite." (A36 30) By combining the greatest possible concreteness with the greatest possible universality of meaning, it becomes an epiphany of the mystery of Being. (A30 225) The greater this power of uniting within itself similar diversities, the brighter the light that breaks forth from its depths and thus the greater its witness to the mysterious light of Being. (A36 32) A form requires this light for its existence and it can be seen for what it is only when it reveals this mystery. The participation of beings or forms in an endless, formless reality and their revelation of that reality is the major theme of classical metaphysics. Plato, unlike Aristotle, insists that forms can be under-

2

stood only when they are seen to participate or bathe in the light of the un-hoped-for and the unapproachable. (A36 164f) Gustav Siewerth refers to the heart of Thomas Aquinas' thought as this insight into the dependence of forms on Being. By recognizing that Being is more than form he made his decisive correction on Aristotle. He saw that Being is not imprisoned by the essences but is the inexhaustible common act in which all things participate and commune with each other. It is deeper and more interior than form. (1) Dante translates into poetry Thomas' reverence for Being's revelation in finite from through his eternal devotion to Beatrice. Her finite form leads him into paradise, to the very throne of God. (A32 435) Pascal emphasizes the finite figure's need for an infinite medium in order to be understood. (A32 555) In his natural scientific writings Goethe speaks of the appearance of the glory of perfect Being in all natural forms. (A36 32, 706ff) The poet Hopkins refers to form as the "inscape" of things, by which he denotes not a static form but the form as it is being released from its creative spring, and yet tightly held together by it. Here lies the focus of the form whence the splendor of Being radiates. The totality of the form can be perceived only from the perspective of infinity. (A32 732)

Natural and human scientists, therefore, can grasp a form exactly only if they are open to the limitless, undefinable, mysterious horizon within which it exists. They must see the horizon that stretches from the being's incomprehensible origin to its incomprehensible goal. (A10 167ff; A30 429; B156 694f; A36 705f, 714f) Thus they must constantly vacillate between the particular comprehensible form and its ground in the incomprehensible infinite. (A10 206ff; 232ff; A31 154ff) Because of this vacillation the mind always knows more than it can express in logical formulations, proofs, concepts and theories. (A36 168) Mystery remains the ground and fruit of rational knowledge. As rationality deepens so too the sense of mystery. (A30 179f, 237) The passive intellect constantly gazes beyond the definitions and limitations established by the active intellect. Therefore, when the mind comprehends anything it comprehends it as ultimately incomprehensible. At all times it must vacillate between the desire for control through system and the desire to wonder at the inconquerable. Ultimately, however, "the 'conquering' side of thought subordinates itself to the 'humble' side; the ordering powers of thought place themselves totally in the service of the inconquerable; the brilliant art of clarifying, ordering and penetration become techniques and tools for allowing the elusive and ungraspable to appear as clearly as possible. (F58 8ff) The ultimate task of thought is not to acquire control over the world according to the formula "abstract and conquer" but to gather together the multiple into a limited form and perceive the limitless light that it emits. (C25 186)

The purpose of this gathering together is to give a new unique meaning and necessity to the components. Meaning and necessity are contained in the form and

---

(1) Gustav Siewerth, <u>Schicksal der Metaphysik von Thomas bis Heidegger</u>, Einsiedeln 1959 pp 375ff

solely in the form. How great their dependence on form is can be seen clearly in a musical composition where a single note or theme receives a radically new significance when placed within the context of a symphony. Once the composer has placed it there it becomes an integral and necessary part of the whole. He alone is entitled to change it and then only at the cost of changing the entire symphony. Likewise an isolated "personality trait" or "social trend" or "cultural influence" receives a new meaning when seen as the integral component of a unique personality, of a unique human form. It too cannot be removed without altering the whole. The force that constitutes this inner necessity and unity of a form is its "inner-form," interiority, or soul that expresses itself by altering the physical appearance of the form. (A36 277) The poet Hopkins describes this "inner form" as an "instress" in the objects, by which he means the "profound unique act that grounds, unites and encompasses the form." (A32 732) This spiritual force is the ultimate measure of each and every form. Because every form does have this measure of its own, the imposition of an alien measure like human need as its definitive meaning will obscure rather than reveal its depths. (A36 31)

Beauty

We have seen how the tension between _morphe_ and _eidos_ reveals the tension within every form between the infinite and the finite, between existence and essence. We must now recognize that this tension within form designates the very essence of beauty. Beauty itself is amorphous but is known as beauty only when it reveals itself in a formed object. (A36 276) Beauty is the "splendor of form as it falls on proportionate and defined elements of matter." (A36 347ff) It is "the flash and dynamic splendor of the hidden, powerful depths of an essence in an expressive form." (A32 9) It is "the transparency through all appearances of the mysterious background of Being." (A10 213) Beauty is the result of Being's need for essence and of essence's need for Being. Both depend on each other for self-realization. Thus there is an order and proportion between them that rests at the very foundation of reality. Because all reality inevitably participates in and reveals this order and proportion, there is a beauty in all things. This fundamental proportion beckons man to an act of faith in the ultimate, eschatological beauty of all that is.

Being's beauty compels this faith by its ability to reveal itself actively, to show itself in an objective being to a subjective being and to call the subjective being to itself. Every beautiful form fascinates by its giving and by its calling. "The form is beautiful only because the pleasure it causes is grounded in the readiness of the depths of the truth and goodness of all reality to show and give themselves as endlessly and inexhaustibly valuable and fascinating. The appearance as the revelation of the depths of reality is at once both the real presence of the depths and of the whole as well as a real witness beyond itself to these depths." (A30 111)

Being is not dead passive matter standing at man's disposal, but as philosophers from Plato to Heidegger have seen, it is light that actively shines and illuminates. The ancients spoke of Being as _physis_ which is derived from the same root as _phainesthai_, to appear. Medieval philosophy spoke of it as radiant light, as

4

manifestabilitas, that opens itself the same way life and mind open themselves.
(A36 331ff) This active, appearing, expressive character of being, "can be called
the 'word' of Being if one understands it as an annunciation that is beyond all that
has been or can be formulated in speech. It witnesses to the source of all annunciation
and therefore to the source of the ability to speak as well." (A36 962) The Greek word
for the glory of Being, kalon, shows that this word-character is especially rooted in
the glory of Being, for its root is kalein, which means to call. Augustine and Leibniz
and Malebranche in speaking of Being as light interpret this light as a word. (A30 155,
274, A36 816) Similarly Gadamer brings out the affinity of light and word by relating
the neo-platonic metaphysics of light with his own and Heidegger's understanding of
language. (2) For Heidegger beings are words in the language of Being. The word of
Being is an evocation, a "ringing silence" that resounds out of the polarity of essence
and existence and makes all human speech possible. (A36 775ff) Both the later Schelling and the later Fichte laid great emphasis on this calling, determining, active
character of Being. Perhaps nothing is so characteristic of Balthasar's philosophical
thought as this emphasis on the primacy of Being's coming out to meet the subject
over the subject's going out in search of Being. (A10 242ff) Being's raison d'être is
its revelation, explication, interpretation of itself in beings; Being's function is the
revelation of its depths. (A10 125ff, 205ff) As will be seen below, Ebeling through
his closeness to Luther and Heidegger also emphasizes the word character of all
reality and of all experience. (cf below p. 47ff.)

The Loss of Wonder

Without this active self-revelation of fathomless mystery in a finite form
there can be no metaphysical wonder and thus neither philosophical nor theological
aesthetics. For this reason it will be valuable to ask why our own age all but completely lost its sensitivity to the mystery and splendor of Being.

The simple amazement and wonder at the mysteriousness and splendor of
Being has been methodically excluded by all the natural sciences and in most cases
by the human sciences. The sciences do not see any need to waste time asking why
a particular object is at all or to be amazed at the mere fact that it is. The scientist
is driven on not by metaphysical wonder but by at best a delight in the endless com-
plexity and order of the universe. This order does not point beyond itself to an endless richness of meaning and mystery.

The attempt to trace briefly the origins of this contemporary metaphysical
blindness will lead past a number of philosophers whom Balthasar himself discusses
only briefly and only in order to make this particular point. There is obviously a
great deal more that could and should be said about these thinkers and the specialist

---

(2) Hans Gadamer, Wahrheit als Methode, Tuebingen 1960, p. 457f

will regret a certain one-sidedness. Nevertheless it is possible and valuable to "use" these thinkers to illustrate a crucial development in Western thought.

The narrowness of the scientific method can be seen in a dualism that divides reality into mind and matter by attributing all spontaneity to the mind and defining matter as purely passive, atomized material for the mind's creative activity. The mind is not principally a contemplator of forms that are unable to explain their own existence, rather a force that constructs its own world. Traces of this dualism can be found in almost all philosophers, but a special impetus towards its explication and dominance in modern philosophy can be seen in the influence of the Arabian Averoes on scholastic philosophy. The Averoists identify the real by which they mean particular things with the rational and attribute to it the same necessity as that of reason's deductions, i.e. of logic. The laws of his thinking and the reality of his idea are identified with reality and given total domination over it. (A36 372) For Duns Scotus, therefore, Being or reality is the emptiest, totally undefined and unlimited concept or category. Because it lacks all specification, the concept of being can be applied univocally to all other concepts and therefore to all other essences because concepts and essences are the same. Because the concept of being is itself indifferent, no differentiation in the world can be attributed to a uniqueness of being in each thing or to a hierarchy of Being but solely to the essential concepts, the haecceitates. Understanding an individual being, therefore, demands sole concentration on the universal essence under which it is subsumed, on its whatness; that it is and why it is are irrelevant. (A36 377ff) Occam draws a logical conclusion when he denies these universal essences and reduces reality to individual things, to valueless, opaque atoms that cannot give information about their origin and purpose. They do not participate in a common act of Being. He makes the metaphysical question about the why of their existence unanswerable for philosophy and demands that the particular thing simply be taken as a given. He reserves to pure Christian faith alone the ability to know the origin and destiny of things in God.

Suarez two centuries later goes behind Occam and revives the Scotist identification of what is with what is thought. The "real" world of thought is thus walled off from the "unreal" "outer world" and involved solely in the game of analyzing and synthesizing concepts, of uniting the subject's thinking with its ideas. Although these "real" ideas are to be thought of as existent outside in the world, that world itself can be neither thought nor located. The outside world is "unreal" and achieves reality only in the "real" concepts in the mind. Thus the Copernican revolution has already taken place: the real world in not primarily the things in themselves but the things as they appear to the mind. Without any analysis of aposteriori evidence the mind makes an original apriori synthetic judgment that being is nothing other than the emptiest of concepts. By attaching this concept to other concepts one creates reality. If the mind is able to do this, it is enabled to construct a "real" world by means of further judgements of the same kind. This initial judgement that reality and its truth are contained only in clear and distinct ideas must be verified and verification is achieved by reflection on the self, on the res cogitans. The "thinking thing" need not and cannot go outside itself to compare its ideas with the material things "outside". Ultimately it is guaranteed by the archetypal divine intellect which it either participates in (Descartes) or is identical with (Spinoza--Idealists). The "unreal" world outside is reduced to purely passive, colorless, valueless material to be manipulated by the mind.

Kant accepts the world as such and describes a pure reason that receives from the "thing in itself" in the outside world a timeless, spaceless, formless impression upon which it imposes its own categories. All meaning and truth are derived from the categories while the thing in itself and its form remain cloaked in inaccessible darkness. Because the aesthetic faculty of judgement is likewise unable to penetrate the darkness, the particular form is unable to reveal its participation in the infinitude of Being. Ultimately, therefore, beauty is reduced to a senseless, valueless, pleasurable relation of subjective capacities. When the unreality of this fantastic world of the subject is finally discovered by Feuerbach, the only existence left is that of the outside world of matter. Thus the materialist is left alone with his totally opaque matter which can in no way be a medium of the transcendent splendor of Being and even less so of the divine splendor. (A36 972)

At the root of this inability to distinguish existence and essence, stretching from the Averoists to the materialists lies the inability to perceive form. Form is misunderstood in two ways. It is seen either as a sign or as a construct that is to be "explained" by analysis.

The Greek tragedians were well aware that the forms they presented on the stage were not merely signs that pointed away from themselves to an absent signified Being. They understood their forms sacramentally; the symbolized was present and appeared effectively in the form. (A36 99) Plato and Plotinus began to weaken this understanding by interpreting the concrete individual form or symbol, i.e. the "thrown-together" more as an "al-legory", as a "talking about something else." (A30 18) For them the really real does not appear in the form, the light of Being does not break forth from the midst of the form, rather the form points away from itself to the light that shines down on it from above; the content is not in the form but only behind it. (A30 144ff; A32 9) Ebeling recognizes this fallacy and points to a sacramental presence of the infinite "in, with and under" the finite. (3)

The other misunderstanding of form arises from the nominalist tradition that was just described. (A36 381) It considers the form primarily in terms of the atoms and forces which constitute it and of the conditions which allowed these constituents to be ordered in a certain way. (A32 18ff) The unique reality of the form is not perceived, for the real is considered to rest only in these conditions and constituents. The form is not understood; it is "explained". Thus Newton explains all forms in terms of physical laws (A36 713) and Kant shows how this is possible by rooting the laws not in the forms but in the categories of the subject. Physics explains forms in terms of subatomic particles; chemistry, in terms of molecules and Jungian psychology in terms of archetypes. (A24 343; A30 481f) Sociology and history reduce the

---

(3) Ebeling, Theologische Sprachlehre, Tuebingen 1972 p. 246

social and individual forms to political, economic and cultural forces that constitute them. (A30 448) Historical literary criticism pursues the biographical influences that explain the form of an author's work. (A30 29) The forms of the gods are explained by the "science" of religion as personifications and projections.

As indispensible as all of these sciences are, they are nevertheless secondary. Without Herder's (A30 78ff) and Goethe's (A36 706ff) morphological methods, without the Gestalt-psychology of Christen von Ehrenfels and without something like Hopkin's (A32 730) eye for "inscape" and "instress" the analytical sciences cannot find the reality they are searching for. Herder, protesting against Kant, claims that a "philosophy of seeing, of evidence, of sign, and experience" is more important and original than every "demonstration" which is only an "exchange of words, a relation of certain concepts." "Evidence and certitude," he says, "must lie in the things . . . in the whole, unsplintered 'depth-feeling' of things or they lie nowhere." (A30 81) "The starting point for the understanding of the world lies not in construing but in looking." "The scientist must have an eye for the qualitative plus of the all-encompassing whole over its parts, which means that a philosophic or artistic eye is indispensable for the 'exact' perception of the thing as it is." (A36 713ff) Goethe sought with his morphology to unite exact sober research with a continual vision of the whole that reveals itself only to the reverent, poetic-religious eye. (A36 705) Our modern eye needs to regain the ability to look at the part in the light of the whole, instead of simply the whole in terms of the part. (A 30 22f) It must regain the vision of fully unique, unrepeatable forms instead of concentrating solely on that which can be universally verified by repeatable experiments. Modern artists and viewers should see in the art work its communion with everything that is, so that they are drawn by it into the infinite origin of all beings. Art and art criticism can help to free the modern eye of the blindness to forms that is preventing it from seeing the divine-human form of Christian revelation. (A30 430, A36 786, A40 268, B156 694f)

Contingent and Absolute Being

Thus far in the discussion of contemplation we have been concerned to show that the vision of absolute splendor presupposes the perception of form. The perception of form in turn presupposes an insight into the distinction between essence and existence. In beholding the form of a particular being the contemplative must perceive its participation with all other beings in a common act of Being. These distinctions between an essence and its actual existence as well as between a particular existant and its participation in the mystery of Being must be made by anyone who is to understand the revelation that Christ is. Any of the varieties of essentialism that were just discussed will inevitably blind man to the splendor of Christ's form.

Once these differences have been recognized the question that now arises is whether or not Being itself participates in a reality greater than itself. Does Being itself have an origin and a destiny? The most powerful witness to such a grounding reality lies in the freedom and gracefulness of the ordered relation of essence and existence. To the contemplator of forms it becomes obvious that the universe is not subjected to an iron law of necessity but that everything could be different or could even not be at all. He comes to see the entire world of forms as barely a slice out of the fullness and richness of Being in which it participates. His imagination portrays for him an infinity of other forms and whole other worlds that could be derived from Being. Being need not reveal itself in the particular shape of this daffodil or that humming bird or this particular girl, but it does. The scientist can tell how their specific forms evolved but he cannot explain ultimately why they evolved; he cannot give them any absolute necessity. They have no inner-worldly purpose that could totally explain and justify their existence. They could just as well not be; the world could carry on without them and yet they are. What they reveal of Being is ultimately a fully gratuitous gracious gift to the recipient.

If this freedom did not exist and Being were forced to assume particular forms in order to fulfil particular goals, the universe would be one huge, fantastically well calculated machine but lack all grace and splendor. (A40 14, A36 950f) Every being would be of interest only as a function of the machine; it would have no freedom, dignity or graciousness of its own. (A36 965) One can see in the example of a dancer that she is not graceful if her movements are not free and done simply to delight those who watch her. Ultimately she is not carrying out any necessary function or fulfilling any ethical need; she freely gives herself and is freely received by her spectators.

This same kind of gracefulness can be seen in the relation of essence and existence and it points to a playfulness and freedom at the heart of Being itself. Yet Being seems to be dependent on essences for its full realization. It looks to the determinacy of form to give stability, meaning, goodness and beauty to its chaotic formlessness. Because of this dependence it would seem that the relation of Being to beings is not ultimately one of graciousness but of necessity. Being cannot hold to itself but is compelled to define, concretize and express itself in beings. If, therefore, one does perceive a freedom and gracefulness at the heart of Being, he must recognize that it cannot be grounded simply in Being.

The gift freely and gracefully given by every contingent being must arise ultimately out of a groundless grace that is totally sufficient to itself. There is no way to keep the freedom and grace of the daffodil, the humming bird or the girl from being crushed in the treads of mechanism, essentialism, determinism or evolutionism except by grounding them in a Being that is the identity of absolute freedom and absolute necessity. It must be grounded in a divine Being who does necessarily what he does freely and does freely what he does necessarily. (A10 272ff) Just as the graceful movement of the dancer must be grounded in her relatively free decision and ability, so the grace of all beings must be grounded ultimately in the absolutely free decision of God. Only because of his decision does the world in any way have to be the way that it is; his freedom is the source of all necessity. (A10 274, A31 129) His decision in turn is determined only by his own wisdom and omnipotence, which are the source of the good he decides to reveal and share. He is compelled by his own goodness alone to give to the essences what he decides is proper for them. (A36 363ff) Plato and Plotinus caught a glimpse of this absolute freedom in their sun of goodness that radiates its light without envy. (A29 364) The sun allows its light to radiate in formed creatures purely out of love for its own beauty, out of the desire to multiply its love by communicating similarity with itself: "Ex pulchro provenit esse omnibus existentibus." (A36 369) His beauty is the ultimate ground of all that is; it is our origin and our destiny.

Just as this gracefulness and freedom in the depths of Being can be accounted for only by recognizing the contingency of Being on an uncreated, fully self-sufficient freedom, so too the basic order and proportion between essence and existence points to the contingency of created Being on a divine intelligent source of order. Undifferentiated Being cannot have the intelligence to create the complex balance and proportion that appears in the universe. The beauty of the universe in its oderliness and graciousness reveals an Absolute Being as its ground.

Immanence

The power of beauty reveals the immanence of the Absolute in all forms. This immanence has been recognized throughout history. It appears in the sacramental light that pours forth from the anthropomorphic gods and goddesses of ancient Greece. (A36 44f, 86, 97, 127) For Plato the analogy between material and spiritual numbers reveals the immanence of divine beauty. (A36 109ff) Benedict clearly sees the presence of the Absolute splendor in the splendor of fraternal love. (A36 302ff) Augustine's notion of the hierarchy of Being implies that the Absolute is the life of all living things and the mind of all minds. Maximus the Confessor (A31) is the first to point explicitly to contingent Being as mediating the immanence of Absolute Being in all beings. (156, 170) Instead of following the Platonic tradition which regards this presence of the Absolute in the sensible singular as a deminution of the Absolute's splendor, Maximus sees the diversity of the corporal, finite individuals as nourishing and enriching the splendor of the Absolute. The finite gives concreteness to divine unity that enriches its splendor. (157f) Maximus finds evidence that the splendor of the Absolute is actually present in the finite by contemplating the beauty of the finite. He sees the Absolute as the immanent ground of the differentiation, the generic unity and the ontological unity of things. Without these, beings would have no beauty.

Thomas Aquinas recognizes the immanence of Absolute splendor when he sees that every being is a proportion or free suspension between essence and existence and that this proportion in turn is freely suspended within the proportion between contingent and absolute Being. Thomas calls this delicate relationship proportionalitas which is a central term of his entire metaphysics and especially of his aesthetics. By virtue of this proportionalitas contingent Being becomes transparent to Absolute Being so that all forms become "glimmers of divine knowlege in things."

Cusanus, Hoederlin, Goethe and Heidegger strive to maintain a similar transparency of the cosmos to the immanence of the Absolute but the sensitivity to this splendor has attenuated rapidly with the rise of technology, urban culture and the increased ability to control reality. Only with great difficulty is man able to behold a form as a "gathering together and unification in the service of the One which presents and expresses itself." (A32 9) Balthasar nevertheless continues to maintain that the very reality of things is their symbolism (A10 223), their revelation of their mysterious interiority and thereby of God. (A10 68ff, 82f) The world is a "magnificent symbol of the divine essence that expresses and reveals itself in parables." (A10 221)

Transcendence

Yet even though contingent Being can mediate the revelation of divine immanence in the universe, the divine must reveal itself primarily in parables or even paradoxes because it is totally other than the universe. Only because of this total otherness does Cusanus dare to call God the Not-Other: he is totally other to such an extent that he is beyond our notion of otherness. (A36 510ff) The name "non-being" therefore can be even more fitting than that of Absolute Being. (A31 81ff)

Because of this otherness the splendor of the Absolute appears only as simultaneously distancing itself. All man can do is reach out for it as it withdraws from his grasp. It appears as the non-appearing and it is this non-appearing that Thomas tries to demonstrate in his five proofs for God's existence. He knows that the heart of God remains hidden in mystery. (A36 354ff) The splendor of the Absolute, therefore, as it appears in the splendor of contingent being is primarily mysterious; all that we know of it is grounded in the abyss of all that we neither are nor grasp. (A32 557) Thus its true essence appears to us only as we are plunged deeper into darkness. (A32 187ff) The more we know him, the more incomprehensible he becomes. For this reason Sophocles, the Father of negative theology, speaks of the gods giving their witness through their hiddenness and distance; their lightless light is the night. (A36 117ff)

Although the analogy of freedom between contingent and absolute Being prevents this appearance from being pure terror, (A36 928f) the analogy must still remain rooted in the "ever-greater dissimilarity" emphasized in the Lateran Council. The dissimilarity is so great that Thomas can say there is no proportion. (A36 355, 367) By no means is the proportion between contingent and absolute Being to be interpreted as establishing a common measure between the two in the all embracing, neutral, empty concepts that Scotus regards as Being. (A31 84) An unbridgeable chasm sunders contingent from Absolute Being because contingent Being arises out of nothingness; it participates in the Absolute only as not participating. (A31 147, 164) This chasm makes of the Absolute's appearance a faceless, formless, colorless, flowing light, (A36 113ff, 238) a light wind that can never be grasped in itself. (A31 78) His beauty is so indescribable that we are forced by it beyond all thinkable, sensible, and graspable forms. (A32 350f, A31 164f) Although his beauty appears in them, it still lies beyond all beauty, number, proportion and measure. (A36 563)

For this reason its appearance is not restricted to "beautiful" forms but can reveal itself in the greatest ugliness. Plato shows that splendor radiates from the ugliness and weakness of Socrates who commits himself totally to the truth, ceases to appear just and is subjected to mockery, scourging and crucifixion. (A36 156ff) Likewise Dostoyevsky portrays the beauty of the Idiot who made the fatal decision to commit his whole life to an idea. (A36 535ff) The criterion of the true splendor is the ability to express itself in such ugliness. (A36 976 cf Parcifal A36 503ff, Erasmus 513ff, Grimmelshausen 528ff) Because the modern science of aesthetics has not known a beauty that can do so, its understanding of beauty has been placed radically in question. (A36 928) Only a "totally other" absolute splendor can appear in the form of one who has succumbed and been broken by the extreme threats to its existence. (A36 140) Out of the smashed shell only divine beauty can emerge like a ripe fruit. (A36 98)

The Loss of Transcendence

Because the vision of transcendent splendor inevitably yanks man out of his trusted world into a strange, frightening, new existence, he naturally seeks in every way possible to prevent himself from being fascinated and possessed by it. Rather than accept the precarious distance between knower and form that aesthetics demands, the tendency is to seek an original unity and to regard all differentiation and formation as at best a passing phase. Monism is the omnipresent threat to all theological aesthetics. The order, balance, proportion and mystery that ground aesthetics are all swallowed up by monism of the spirit, by the limitless self-knowledge of a limitless Mind. The monism of matter that we live with today was the inevitable result of the monism of the spirit. Because it is the supreme threat to any theological aesthetics, it will be necessary to trace briefly its development in modern thought.

It was prepared for by the later Plato who in the _Timaeus_ and the possibly pseudonymous _Epinomis_ reduces all Being to the cosmic reason, i.e. to the order in the universe that reason can perceive. This reduction is further developed by Aristotle and flourished in the Stoic notion of _logos spermatikos_. Human reason is called upon to identify itself with this cosmic-divine reason either by ecstatically expanding its soul to the dimensions of the world-soul or by seeking mystical union between God and the divine spark that is its soul. In both cases the finite self is to be destroyed and dissolved into the infinite self. (A36 197-225) Dun Scotus greatly furthers the reduction when in his attempt to distinguish philosophy and theology he denies to philosophy the ability to know God and designates as its formal object his notion of Being as the emptiest concept. In the dark night of the late medieval situation it is readily possible for Scotus to emphasize the inability of the cosmos to reveal God to unaided reason and then for him to fall back on an anti-contemplative practical theology and a non-understanding, pure faith for the only possible knowledge of God. Occam is even more radical in the sundering of reason and faith. Suarez, however, in the age of rationalism has greater faith in the power of reason and restores God as the formal object of philosophy. He retains nevertheless the Scotist notion of Being as the emptiest possible concept, which means that philosophy is enabled to wing itself up beyond God to Being and from that perspective to look down into God's essence and his creative and redemptive action. In this same sphere of Being, beyond God, reason is also enabled to synthesize a priori worldly essences and declare them real simply by virtue of their determination to being, their ordo ad esse.

This identification of Being with the concepts of a supremely creative mind prepares the way for a communion of the mind with God without the mediation of form and its revelation of Being. Once man no longer needs to depend on the sensible, the spatial and the temporal, for his knowledge, his aesthetics will inevitably be sundered from his search for truth. He no longer needs to develop a sense for order, shape and proportion to know the Absolute.

This awareness of an immediate knowlege of the Absolute is greatly furthered by the German fourteenth century mystic, Meister Eckhart. (A36 390ff) Eckhart's prime intention is to attribute the splendor of creation entirely to God. He is eminently aware of God coming to him in all Being and interprets it as the birth of the Son from the Father in the medium of creation. He is equally aware of his own coming from God and interprets that as his being born with the Son out of the Father. Creation has its ground and goal in Christ and in his redemption so that every creature is rooted in this its highest uncreated fulfillment. Man is enabled to receive this gift of Being from God only by his Gelassenheit, i.e. his total openness and receptivity. The soul must allow itself to be so humiliated and impoverished by God that it is completely empty, for only then can God fill him and be born in him. This is not a Stoic indifference to pain and pleasure but an openness to whatever God may send. It is love that breaks through all created things to behold God in them. Eckhart's mystical vision of God is so overwhelming to his impoverished, passive self that the self appears to be robbed of all its own being and goodness. Because all goodness always comes from God and remains outside of the soul, its goodness is like a light in the air, an image in the mirror, or a cloak placed over a slave. The soul is too insignificant to achieve any goodness of its own or to participate in any way in God's goodness. Nothing created is good.

His difficulties arise in attempting like Origen to explain his insights in terms of an inadequate philosophy. Operating with the neo-Platonic emanation-return schema he interprets the derivation of Being and of himself from God as their emanation from the divine identity and he interprets his experience of God's birth in himself as his return to divine identity. Moreover, his intimate, personal knowledge as a Christian of God's interiority leads him to seek beyond the Trinitarian differentiation a point of perfect unification in the truest being of God, in his free intellect. The birth of God in man is then interpreted as the birth of free intellect in man; man's reason is an uncreated divine spark. Since according to Thomas truth rests primarily in the intellect and goodness in things, Eckhart considers Being to reside authentically in the divine intellect and in its sparks whereas it resides in things as having fallen away from its original authenticity. Things outside of reason are non-being and must be gathered back into the intellect. Having thus identified Being with the divine intellect and its sparks, he regards the creatures as non-being and darkness. The task of the creature, therefore, is to become aware of his own and all creatures' non-being and thereby leave it behind. Then the divine spark in him, his uncreated reason, can be united with the divine intellect. Thus Eckhart's attempt to express Christian receptivity and selflessness philosophically culminates in an identification of God and Being in the form of an Indian pantheism. The identification is accomplished by means of a radical intensification and personalization of the neo-Platonic emanation-return schema in the light of his profound

Christian faith. This Christianized schema is his most important bequest on the Idealists.

Idealism remains in all its phases an interpretation of Kant and thus revolves around the transcendental act-structure of the thinking and acting subject. It is unleashed by Schiller who identifies the things that Kant tried to keep apart: the phenomenon and the thing-in-itself, the infinite and the finite intellect, the should and the will. These identifications allow man to assume God's place as the master of Being. (A36 848) It might be said to draw the conclusion from Scotus' equation of Being with a concept and thus with the mind itself on the one hand and Eckhart's equation of Being and God on the other. The unavoidable conclusion is to interpret the supremely free, creative mind as God. Luther contributed to this identity by attributing Being to God and non-being to the creature along with Eckhart. This inevitably evoked the creature's revolt and its appropriation of Being to itself and non-being to God. (A36 374f)

The basic movement in the Idealism these thinkers evoked can be seen by concentrating on the Mind and seeing how all that could be thought of as above the Mind, i.e. God and Being, is absorbed into the Mind (God becomes man) and how all that is below the Mind, i.e. world and nature, is totally caught up in an evolutionary process that has its origin in the Mind, exists solely for it and is destined to be reabsorbed by it (Man becomes God). This is an absolutizing of human freedom and reason and is thoroughly dependent on the overwhelming dimensions opened to human freedom and knowledge by Christianity. (A36 406) Like Eckhart Fichte (A36 879ff), Schelling (A36 890ff) and Hegel (A36 904ff) all revolve around the Christian dogma that the human and the divine are united in the Son of God and that all Christians are called to participate in the divine nature as sons of God. The unique historical person of Christ becomes increasingly irrelevant but the Christological dogmas are closely worked over for their anthropological relevance. They are interpreted to mean that God can become God and fully realize himself only in becoming man and entering non-being. This happens when man fully realizes himself by overcoming the non-being that limits his freedom and knowledge and thereby becoming God. This process of God becoming man differs decisively from the neo-Platonic schema of emanation and return in that it is not grounded in a boundless graceful freedom. The divine Mind lies under a necessity to fulfil itself by seeking differentiation in nature and in human minds.

If God is compelled to create or emanate the world, Being is robbed of the freedom that makes transcendental aesthetics possible. Robbed of its freedom Being is likewise robbed of its mystery, for it now becomes possible to explain exactly why everything is at all and why it is the way it is. Without freedom and mystery Being can hardly be called beautiful or witness to a transcendent splendor.

It is important, therefore, to consider more closely how and why absolute necessity was conceived to be the ground of Being. The Idealists demonstrate this by designating three different stages in God's existence. The first stage is his absolute identity with himself as an unreal, ideal, individual essence totally unrelated to the human cogito. Schelling and the later Fichte call this stage "Being" or the unconscious part of God. God realizes himself in the second stage by contracting himself into worldly forms and thereby plunging himself into multiplicity and non-identity. Through this _kenosis_ he becomes the ground of all beings, the essence of all essences who is related to the individual essences as Christ is related to all men. Just as man lives only in Christ so too essences are dead in their abstract individuality, and alive only insofar as their very existence already implies their being assumed into unity with God. God is angered by their abstract imprisonment in individuality and longs for the overcoming of all duality. The human _cogito_ frees God from his imprisonment by integrating all multiplicity into itself and thus fusing infinite and finite life. This fusion is the third stage of God's existence. In Hegel's early theological writings the unification is a movement of love, that begins with God's free emptying of himself and his identification with what is alien to himself. This leads to the breaking of his heart in his death on the cross and through such an act of love to the freeing of the individuals from their individuality so they may return to unity within the whole. The negation within God, his weakness and death, mediate the integration. When, however, the later Hegel thoroughly formalizes the historical cross into a "speculative Good Friday," the unification it effects is no longer one of love but of absolute knowledge. The cross is reduced to the ever-recurring clash between thesis and antithesis that results in the "resurrection" of a new unity in a synthesis. The ultimate synthesis by the Mind is God's coming to know and realize himself perfectly. Being, therefore, ceases to be mysterious and God is so completely caught up in this implication/complication schema that he is deprived of all freedom and transcendence. God is fully reduced to his immanent role as the divine spark and the depths of the Mind, and man is exalted to the dignity of the Holy Spirit. He is the ultimate source of all splendor in the universe. Therefore, to know this splendor no longer requires that man begin and end with the contemplation of finite forms but that he come to know himself. Thus the ever-disappearing, elusive splendor is replaced by the splendor of human fulfillment.

This same splendor of man in his divine creativity is seen by another tradition to rest more in man's erotic, poetic heart than in his reason. This is the tradition of poets ranging from the Renaissance to Goethe, Hoelderlin, Rilke and Heidegger who seemingly turn once again to the world of forms and more specifically the forms of ancient Greece as mediators of a cosmic splendor. This "Mediation of the Ancients" (A36 593ff) is an attempt to maintain a transparency of the cosmos to divine splendor in the face of an increasingly imageless, visionless philosophy and a disintegrating Christian culture. It calls upon Western man to remain in touch with the childhood vision, the archetypal experience of Being that he had in Greece. Like the individual adult, our whole culture in order to survive must regain and reappropriate its original experience.

Nevertheless, the splendor or light of Being is still much less the initiator that breaks from the depths of a form than it is the light cast by the heroic eros of the poet's heart. Particular forms at best serve to ignite the poet's eros but he is soon able to leave them behind and concentrate on the splendor of his own enthusiasm. This contemplation of his own eros becomes his relation to the Absolute. His receptive, responsive prayer is replaced by an autonomous soliloquy and his practice of religion by his practice of art. Art transforms the cosmos by endowing it with "divine" splendor and mystery. In Heidegger's terms the poet is the new prophet and saint who alone can hear the voice of Being and through his art reveal to the rest of mankind the presence of the "foured": the mortal and the immortal, the heavenly and the earthly. Because he alone has within him the idea of the highest beauty, he alone can redeem the image of nature. He leads the cosmos to its fulfillment by drawing it through his art into the creative, Titanic, divine presence of his genius and inspiration. The creative task of this godly eros turns the eros inevitably into suffering by requiring of the poet and lover heroic asceticism and self-sacrifice. His heroic struggle against an increasingly opaque, materialistic and threatening cosmos is transported into a transcendent sphere. This is the meaning of such "mythic" figures as Don Juan, Faust, Zarathustra and Rilke's absolute artist.

The human eros proves to be no match for this cosmos, however, for the more any kind of transcendence beyond beings to Being and beyond Being to God is denied in psychology, sociology and literature, the more the cosmos becomes Goethe's chud-chewing monster and is subjected to Nietzsche's morbid doctrine of the eternal return. Here are the roots of the twentieth-century heroic pessimism in which the heroic heart revolts against the absurdity of the universe and takes up the task of Sisyphus. Nietzsche's superman, Zarathustra, fuses in his ego supreme happiness and supreme nausea, God and the scoundrel. Thus the glory of Being as a witness to the transcendent Absolute is totally lost and God is declared dead. Heidegger resists this conclusion in a highly poetic attempt to retain a vision of the gracious friendly glory of Being, but for him too this splendor although not confined to the human eros, remains purely immanent. The ontological difference between limitless Being and limited beings is not deepened to the difference between absolute and contingent Being.

As can now be seen, keeping open these ontological differences for the eyes of the contemplative is crucial for any theological aesthetics and an extremely difficult task. Recent Christian theology has abandoned the task for the greater part and in so doing abandoned an essential presupposition for its credibility.

Chapter Two

THE SPIRITUALITY OF EROS

The preceeding chapter on contemplation has attempted to show the necessity of philosophical wonder as a presupposition of theological method and the obligation of theological aesthetics to see that philosophy maintains it. The man who is unable to wonder at the beauty of a spider will be unable to wonder at the splendor of Christ. It was emphasized at the beginning that this act of wonder must be rooted in the heart's integration of intellect, will, emotions, and senses. If then it does arise in the contemplation of form, the vision must involve man's desire, his deed, and his receptivity. Because these three acts are constitutive of wonder, the basic human act, they constitute three basic "spiritualities." The first of these spiritualities is the erotic ascent from a love for finite and relative goodness, truth and beauty to a love for infinite and absolute goodness, truth and splendor. This is a basically Platonic spirituality. The second is more Aristotelian and attempts to eliminate the evil and ugliness that obscures the splendor of Being by actively reforming reality and liberating it to self-communication. The third and more Stoic spirituality is based on man's humble surrender of himself into the control and guidance of the Absolute. No one of these ways may absolutize itself but each must always make room in itself for the other two. (A40 247ff)

The Horizon of Love

The first more Platonic spirituality is based on man's profound desire for something he only vaguely remembers. Almost every culture manifests an awareness that the race and each individual has already enjoyed the height of human fulfillment and that his main task is in some way to return to this state. Man has a heavenly origin in the Garden of Eden and is striving to return to a similar heavenly paradise. The reason for this longing to return to a lost paradise lies in the crucial importance of the mother's love for all personal development. Her love evokes his love as the sunshine evokes the growth of a plant. She allows him to become a loving and knowing subject. Her smile offers him fulfillment as a being that discovers itself in going out of itself and giving itself to a loving thou. (A40 13ff) The otherness of the thou enables the ego to step out into a wondrous reality in which all finite forms speak to it of infinite, absolute love, of a love like Eichendorff's "dark green night," the rustling forest and maternal womb of life out of which we arise and in which we live, move and are. (A40 453) In contemplating the form of her smile the infant comes to understand that it is welcome in existence and that it belongs here. The mother becomes for it an experience of unconditional affirmation, of absolute love. As its first goddess, she transforms for it the horizon of Being into a horizon of love. She enables the infant to draw the entire universe so totally into their love relation that no later experience will ever be able to surpass the horizon she has opened.

The insight into the identity of love and Being is hardly more than a momentary flash as the child soon realizes that its mother is no more than a woefully inadequate image of the Absolute. He soon sees that he cannot embrace the entire universe in his relation to his mother but must find himself a new all-encompassing relationship, a new god. She can no longer be the ultimate source of his identity and meaning in life. The horizon she opened remains, nevertheless, his utopia and his life will be spent trying to draw the universe into a new relation analogous to this initial maternal relation. Just as all the objects that he knew as a child were images of this maternal love and found their meaning and necessity there, so later he will seek to place all beings in relation to his horizon of Being as love. He commits himself as a child to place all that he will ever know into the light of this love and to trace all light back to this mysterious light. (A40 453)

Because this childhood vision and credulity is his closest contact with the infinite and eternal, the longer he can remain faithful to it, the deeper his creativity and his understanding will be. (A36 48) The unlimitedness of the horizon enables him to find the unity and re-lev-ance of all things because he can raise all thing up (relevare) and carry them back (re-late) to this original horizon. In terms of Plato's myth, he is able to remember the world of pure ideas that he once lived in and comes to understand the universe by placing all things in relation to them.

Eros as the Unity of the Transcendentals

Because this horizon is one of love the attempt to understand by drawing all things back to their origin is necessarily an act of love, an erotic desire for the true, good and beautiful. Man achieves his intellectual, ethical and aesthetic fulfillment through the same movement of eros. Therefore, his pursuit of truth must not be sundered from his longing for the good and his admiration of the beautiful.

This unity of the transcendentals was destroyed by the tradition that lost sight of the distinction between essence and existence and therefore lost form and transcendence. Kierkegaard's sundering of the aesthetic and the ethical was a reaction against the decidedly non-transcendent notion of beauty common at his time and derived largely from Kant. Kant's "pure beauty 'abstracts' from all objectivity and every ethical interest in order to enjoy the form in its unrelatedness and isolated meaning disinterestedly and with the pure formal harmony of man's cognitive faculty. This undoubtedly makes Kant the first theoretician of abstract art." (A36 841) The transcendentals no longer commune in a common Being but are aspects of the transcendental structure of reason in its critical self-understanding. They can be seen in their purity only in abstraction from each other. Over against this purely immanent notion of beauty Kant does, however, retain an aesthetic vision of the Good as sublime, as the sublimity of God beyond man's moral sublimity and thus remains standing before the threshold of Idealism. (A36 847) Once the philosophies of identity reject this notion of a transcendent sublime, they are left with Kant's inner-worldly, subjective, abstracted beauty. Kierkegaard must reject any such attempt to absolutize the aesthetic affirmation of Being since it denies the ethical, the real existence of man.

An understanding of the communion of the transcendentals in Being overcomes this false dichotomy. The unity of truth and goodness appears in the Greek word for truth, a-lethia which according to Heidegger means unhiddenness or revelation. This revelation is seen by Plato and Plotinus as Being's selfless giving of itself to and through beings and thus as goodness. The good is the self-communication and enrichment of Being whereby it becomes the source of all value. (A10 209) An object appears within this self-communication of Being first as what it is or is not (as true) and then as something that demands decision and must perhaps be related to myself (as good). (A40 240) "Truth wants to be done just as much as to be seen. This is the true sense of the existential character of truth which one really possesses only when he does it; when he achieves not only a conceptual insight but expresses his entire being and life through it." (A28 251)

There is also an inner unity of beauty and goodness. Zeus expresses mythologically this unity in that he is at once the glorious god and yet the god who overcomes the chaotic, Titanic forces of Mother Earth in order to establish order and justice. In his splendor he is the all-just, all-powerful, divine law in heaven that struggles with man against evil for the establishment of justice. (A36 75ff, 106ff) Likewise, it is precisely the splendor of Sappho's god Eros that causes the earth to shudder and to find its good order. (A36 80ff) Jupiter's splendor is the ground of the fate that sends and accompanies Aeneas as his ethical norm. The Greeks tend in general to draw the beautiful closer to the good than to the true as can be seen in their word kalokagathia. Plato identifies the two and exhorts man to contemplate the beauty and order of the cosmos in order to achieve moral harmony. (A36 184ff) Splendor and goodness are united insofar as they are both grounded in form and thus in God, the formless source of all form. Man's growth in both goodness and beauty is achieved primarily by forming and moderating himself through habits. In that good habits give form they make Being form-osus and speciosus, the Latin words for beautiful. (A36 339ff) Ultimately it is conformation to the same divine form that gives man both his goodness and his beauty. (A32 120ff) They are both reflections of the divine made possible by this conformation. (A32 346, A36 271ff)

Dante brings out the unity of goodness and beauty in philosophy. "The ethical is the beauty of philosophy. Just as the beauty of the body stems from the order and symmetry of its members so too the beauty of ...philosophy stems from the order of the ethical virtues." Since love of the beautiful is the soul of philosophy, "there can be no ethics without beauty. Even less so can there be beauty without ethics since ethics is the highest of the intellectual spheres and borders on the divine. Thus the ethical and the aesthetic are for Dante united in a close embrace." (A32 461) To see the embrace between goodness and splendor is to love the good not because of its usefulness or pleasurableness but because of its splendor, because it freely and graciously grants participation in itself and is thus good in itself. (A10 207ff, A36 339ff, A30 145) The good and the splendid, therefore, far from placing each other in question are interior to one another and co-ordinate axes. (A30 20f)

In order to see the interdependence of the true and the beautiful one must see that truth is Being revealing itself by measuring itself in a form. (A30 587) Man takes his own measure and form through his thought (cogito) which he can do only because he has already been thought (cogitor). Both truth and beauty are grounded in the Absolute Measure that emits and recalls, unifies and simplifies man and all other creatures. All things have both their truth and beauty from this divine measure, from

19

their unhiddenness before the divine intellect. (A10 246ff, A32 120f, A36 280) Thus the light of the Absolute appears in all beings as their measure and deserves as such to be called Absolute Truth and Absolute Beauty. (A32 125ff, A36 344ff) It incorporates the splendor and truth of contingent Being and appears most convincingly and graciously in the symbol. (A10 156)

All three transcendentals, therefore, presuppose and ground one another. Their common source is the light and measure of the Absolute and their common place of appearance is the finite form. "The form is beautiful only because the pleasure it arouses in showing and giving itself grounds the profound truth and goodness of reality itself and thereby allows reality to reveal itself as infinitely valuable and fascinating." (A30 111) Truth and goodness have this fascination because of their beauty, because of the radiance that make them desirable in themselves. (A10 213) Without that radiance truth would lose its power to convince and goodness would lose its attractiveness and Being would lose its preferability over non-being. (A30 15; A36 291) The pursuit of goodness and truth must, therefore, contain an aesthetic moment. In fact aesthetics can arise only where theory and ethics converge. (A30 145, A32 100) No one of the transcendentals can be pursued in separation from the other two, for the pursuit of the transcendentals is ultimately the pursuit of God who is indivisibly one in his truth, goodness, and glory. Because he is their source, their model, and goal - they are simply three different images of his love. (A32 709)

Eros and Self-Realization

Due to this interdependence of the transcendentals one is compelled to recognize with Plato, Plotinus (A36 278, 967), Cusanus (A36 570f) and the early Hegel (A36 908) that the pursuit of truth in thought is inseparable from the erotic quest for goodness and truth. Love and thought must be combined in a common act of wonder. Since no one can know the full truth of any being without placing it in relation to the true-good-beautiful horizon of Absolute Love that was opened to him as a child, there can be no full knowledge without love. (A10 251) Eros enables man to see because the vision of the eye is grounded in the love of the heart. (A30 379) Therefore, the pursuit of truth is identical with the search for ethical and aesthetic fulfillment, with the search for self-realization.

This process of self-realization is inevitably an erotic ascent to the absolute origins of one's understanding. It is a search to become a child again (repuberescere --Augustine A32 108) by seeking a truth whose formal and final cause, whose very meaning and accessibility is love. (A10 93ff, 259f) Self-realization in understanding is due to the eros that compels one from the less to the more real. One ascends from appearances, to finite beings, to infinite contingent Being, to the revelation of Absolute Being. (A32 841, A36 964, A10 97) The greatest temptation is to stop with the discovery of a particular idea, ability, possession or any finite being and to absolutize or divinize it.. If one does so, the inability of such an idol to fulfil the longing aroused by his childhood vision will lead to an ever deepening despair and cynicism. (A10 242) The light of one's eros must be strong enough to love all forms primarily as shadows and footprints of the formless. One must retain a restless heart that constantly drives one beyond what one has grasped. (A36 276)

If eros does at any point succumb to the temptation to absolutize any particular object, it will thrust the lover into a wild vacillation between agony and ecstasy. Michaelangelo and Shakespeare were finally driven by this vacillation to see their beloveds in the light of the true Absolute. (A36 610ff) Giordano Bruno and his long line of successors, however, persisted in identifying the beauty of their beloveds with the splendor of Being and were subjected to such violent disappointments that they finally identified love and hate. (A36 620ff) In the modern novel eros has been so totally robbed of its vertical dimension that it degenerates into perversion and the hatred of the other as hell itself. (A36 750, 940) Likewise contemporary science having lost an eros that searches for a higher truth has degenerated into curiosity and the passion to know more and more facts.

The cause for this death of transcendent eros is the monism brought about by the conceptualism and essentialism described above. The path to its revival lies in the regaining of a love for concrete human existence. Darwin, Marx and Freud have led us along the way towards rediscovering that man is not a mind or an idea but that he exists. He is a physical being who recapitulates the cosmos and remains rooted in it. Eros can ascend to a vision of Absolute Being in all forms of nature if it can see again the bond between itself and nature; if it can see how the human being gathers into itself the whole of the universe and shares with the universe a common act of Being. If eros sees this union on the one hand and man's union with the divine on the other, it will be able to experience again the entire universe as coming from and returning to the Absolute.

The contemplative eros that possesses this twofold vision and turns its attention specifically towards concrete human existence, will see the dependence of human freedom and personality on an Absolute Thou. Since personhood can arise only in response to the goodness of another person, he sees in the very existence of contingent persons the existence of an Absolute Personal Goodness. Any attempt he makes to know the freedom and uniqueness of another's thou demands openness to the Absolute Thou as its source and destiny. Otherwise the knower enslaves the other's freedom under its own limitations and becomes for the other a "hell" that offers him "no exit." Therefore, as the recapitulation of all nature and as dependent on the Absolute Thou, one's fellow man indicates the contingency of the entire universe on the Absolute and compels the contemplative's eros beyond both the macro- and the microcosmos to the Absolute.

The unique conscious openness of the human thou to the Absolute makes human beauty the most exalted reflection of the divine splendor. The erotic ascent to the Absolute began for Pindar, Sappho and Socrates in the contemplation of the beautiful bodies of athletes, warriors, maidens, and boys. The body as the visible expression of the virtue of the heart has a beauty that poets from the Greeks to Hoelderlin, Goethe and Schiller have regarded as the fullest and truest revelation of the splendor of Being. Nothing so enraptures man and brings him closer to the Absolute as the beauty of another person. A remedy for the modern inability to perceive the transparency of cosmic beauty to divine splendor lies, therefore, in a deeper understanding and love for the human person. "Modern man" must listen to the phenomenologists' and personalists' insistence that the fullness of man is profoundly ignored when he is subjected to the myopic, natural-scientific vision of most psychology, sociology and modern art. If he finds this deeper understanding and appreciation for another's uniqueness and freedom, he will also find a new awareness of the personal uniqueness and freedom of the Absolute.

Such a new insight into the personal character of the Absolute will cause the Absolute to appear even more hidden in the cosmos because even more totally other than the non-human cosmos. Nevertheless the cosmos need not lose its transparency again. This new understanding simply means that philosophy must be willing to place intersubjective love at the center of its contemplation of the cosmos. (A24 103-115; A36 973; A40 276f) It must allow eros to regain its childhood vision of unconditional love and to draw the universe with itself back into the original unity. It must resist the refusal of most natural and social scientists to recognize any such metaphysical basis in their undertakings. It must also resist the psychological attempt to control the transcendent movement of eros. Eros must not be turned back in upon itself but allow itself to be possessed by a transcendent other. This is the basic conflict between Jung and Buber and must be resolved in favor of Buber. (A40 251, A30 481f) Only then can self-communication within the interpersonal relationship retain its primacy and become the heart of the spirituality of action.

Chapter Three

THE SPIRITUALITY OF ACTION

Centrality of Communication

The need for a spirituality of action is basically a need for inter-action or communication with others. The ascent of eros has often been tried without this fidelity to others and has frequently resulted in an illusory escape. One cannot ascend to the Absolute alone but must take the entire universe with him, transforming and conforming it to the Absolute. The child is soon robbed of his easy vision of Being's splendor and must struggle with the entire universe to restore its transparency. This chapter will trace how this struggle is rooted in communication of subjects with objects and with other subjects; how one's uniqueness is rooted in this communication and how communication in the languages of Being, words and art has its ground in the Absolute. Without such an attempt to commune with all beings and thereby to free them from their protective shells of drabness and ugliness, they will be prevented from revealing their inner splendor and giving truth its power of conviction. True communication and interaction prevent the methodic search for truth from veering off into escapist isolation or the computation of facts and turns it into an aesthetic act.

The quest for truth must remain a continual back and forth between contemplation and action because the seeker can never fully re-create the world he sees; he can never bridge the gap between essence and existence. (B9 83) The more vivid his childhood vision is, the more obvious the tension between essence and existence and the greater the need to seek both his own and the other's full realization. His naive vision of Absolute Splendor demands that he fulfil himself and the universe. Communication is the path to this fulfillment for communication is the very meaning of existence. Being's splendor is its communication and the ground of its credibility and attractiveness. (A10 246ff) Man can perceive Being only by participating in this self-communication through his aesthetic concern to make himself and his world increasingly transparent to Being's radiance. This concern is the very focal point and meaning of his existence. If he were to refuse the communication of his total self, he would refuse his humanity. Nothing, therefore, can be of greater concern to him than his faith in the ability of Being to reveal itself and in the ability of one's fellow man to receive this revelation. (A10 246) In addition he must trust his own ability to induce with great modesty, reverence and tenderness both object and subjects to reveal their inner form. (A36 234)

Communication Liberates and Creates Uniqueness

All objects require the administration of a subject in order to fully communicate and thus fully realize themselves. By welcoming the thing into his person and humanizing it, the subject must give it the freedom it requires to express itself. The scientist, artist and technician assume this responsibility to a thing when they give it a new form and thus a new meaning. (A10 36, A24 19, 71ff, B58 37f) If this new formation is not to be a distortion but a liberation and a fulfillment, it must not be an arbitrary imposition but a conformation to a divine idea. He must seek to see the thing within the light of its origin and destiny in the Absolute. He must allow it to reveal its most interior depths by drawing it into his own relation to the Absolute. (A10 257ff) The ultimate truth of a thing rests both in the thing itself and in the subject's knowledge of the Absolute; its full realization occurs only in the meeting of the two.

This liberation of objects closely parallels the attempt to liberate subjects by increasing their transparency to the Absolute. The creative activity that one subject exercises on another is his vision of the other in the light of the Absolute, for it is this vision that offers the other the love and freedom he needs to realize himself. This enables him to de-emphasize the faults of the other and to offer him an ideal image of himself. He can offer to the other a much wider horizon and a much deeper hope than someone without this vision. Receiving from the Absolute the freedom to love unconditionally he can serve another by pouring himself out into a particular situation. Through hard, concrete work he can objectify all that is chaotic, subjective, puerile fantasy and abstractness in himself and give it a specific form. (A40 249, A30 15) The form gives him a deeper self-possession, interiority, certitude and freedom. It unifies and particularizes his relations to others, to society, to the universe and to the Absolute. It welds his individual decisions and actions into habits and confers on him a greater simplicity and nobility that manifests itself physically.

As communication gives further definition to the self, it simultaneously deepens his vision of Absolute Splendor and enhances his conformation to it. (A32 173, A36 369) The question arises whether philosophy can comprehend this fusion of increasing uniqueness and increasing universalization. (A36 908ff, B66 5 ff, B58 42ff) This decision determines whether or not a person is willing, on the basis of philosophical evidence, to accept all the restraints that seem to arise from his emersion in a unique love relation. It requires great courage to bindingly entrust oneself to another and to accept from him the norm of ones own existence. Such self-surrender appears to mean the destruction of the self rather than its universalization. Two subjects can find the courage for mutual self-surrender the more clearly they can hear in one another the Absolute calling each to his unique fulfillment. Hearing this call and recognizing the ability of another to reveal uniquely the splendor of the Absolute, places great demands on one's aesthetic sensitivity. Only a keen sensitivity can see how the mystery of each person is guaranteed by their ability to reveal absolute splendor uniquely. Only such sensitivity can see how the unique revelation offers the viewer unique fulfillment and universalization.

A person who is so sensitized has love as his norm and thus finds the patience and reverence to wait for the other to make the right revelation at the right time. He will not indulge in curiosity, spiritual rape or spiritual exhibitionism but cultivates a love that knows when to reveal what must be revealed and when to hide what must remain hidden. Unlike psychiatry such love is not in danger of forcing into the open what should remain hidden. (A10 126ff) On the other hand it has the courage to say what the other does not want to hear and prevents such criticism from causing serious misunderstanding. Both subjects can understand and persuade each other not by intellectual or psychological acumen but by the completeness of their insight. They do not need to judge one another but can simply allow the evidence of their insight to appear and pass judgement itself. (A10 133ff) The judge is the splendor that radiates from the fullness of their insight.

Languages

This communication occurs on various levels and in various languages. The languages of nature, words and art all are grounded in the religious act of responding to the beckoning self-revelation of Being. The infant's self-consciousness arises in this religious response and simultaneously with his ability to express himself in some form of language. Without language man cannot achieve a full understanding of himself or of the world around him. Understanding begins in the perception of a sensible image from which an inner word is derived and this inner word finds fulfillment only in an outer word. Whatever physical mode of expression this outer word may assume, without it his understanding of the word of Being and the form in which it is revealed remains totally inadequate. Because the revelation of Being is one of love, the response to it must be an act of love that is unable to retain for itself what it receives but must pass it on in an outer word. As long as love remains the norm of all knowledge, one cannot communicate something he has already grasped fully but only something that he comes to grasp fully in the act of communication. His understanding achieves its very humanity precisely because it is an act of Being's communication analogous to sexual love. Knowledge is a process of conception, gestation and birth, and if it fails to issue in communication, it is a miscarriage. (A32 623) Socrates, therefore, engages others in dialogue in order to bring their thinking to fruition and calls himself a midwife.

The language of the body plays an essential role in the development of understanding. As a body man necessarily shares in the communicative ability of all other animate and inanimate bodies. Even without his intending to communicate, his very existence as a body means that he automatically expresses Being to others. Like all plants and animals he must express an invisible principle of life. He can also deliberately use his body to convey understanding in gestures, dances and rituals but even these expressions of man's deepest experiences demonstrate his intimate link with nature. (A28 87f) As these expressions become more deliberate, and the body is more thoroughly penetrated by a unique, self-conscious principle of life, its stature, movement, eyes and smile become manifestations of a personal depth. As we saw above, these manifestations can make the body so beautiful that it becomes for others the beginning of their erotic ascent to the Absolute.

The ability of personal beauty to manifest itself is, however, greatly increased by verbal language. Having derived an inner word from a sensible image, man acquires a certain distance from his experience and this frees him to choose a unique outer word to express his unique personal insight. The richness of the language that permits his unique expression mediates the creation of his own uniqueness. If he lets himself be overcome by the conventionality of his language, however, his unique personality will not only never be expressed but never even come into existence. Although he need not thus be overwhelmed by his language, it is inevitable that the style of his language will greatly influence the style of his thought. He must seek to enter a living dialogue with the thinkers and poets who shaped the style of his language and by acquiring a unique relation to these thinkers achieve a unique style of language and thus a unique consciousness. The freedom and uniqueness of his relation to these thinkers and poets will increase the more he can trust them and, as we saw, this trust will grow with the growth of his trust in an Absolute that speks to him and calls him to his unrepeatable fulfillment through others. For this reason his religion is the decisive factor in the development of a unique style of language and thought.

The importance of both religion and a uniqueness of style as well as their interdependence become especially clear in the language of art. All great art manifests a uniqueness of style and the history of art offers convincing confirmation of Goethe's claim that all great art is religious. That art is a matter of the gods was especially obvious in archaic and classical Greek art. The artist drew his inspiration from the gods and his task was either to build an epiphany of a god or else to make offerings for him. (A36 69) Homer shows his religious intent in the portrayal of a deep personal relation between the hero and his god. This emphasis on personality stripped mythological art of its magic and superstition. By praising the hero in his free relation, he praises the freedom of the god who gave the hero his beautiful form. He thereby reveals the divine splendor in the hero's form and inspires the reader to imitation. (A36 47f)

Balthasar sees Greek tragedy as one of the most powerful presentations of divine splendor in art. The tragedians worship the gods by first gathering together in a suffering hero all of the reasons for not believing in the gods and then overcoming these reasons in a final act of faith. The tragedies show in this way the supreme difficulty facing any art work of trying to portray the splendor of god's total otherness, mystery and seeming indifference. The depths of faith required are so great that very few artists will be able to attain and maintain it. Euripides finally abandoned the task of tragedy as suffering man began to appear more splendid than the gods who could not suffer. From that point on classical Greek and Roman art began to limit themselves more and more to a purely immanent ethics. (A36 94ff, 141f, A40 347ff) Much of Western art succumbed to this difficulty in the same way and became increasingly blind to the transcendent. Although as late as the nineteenth century such poets as Hoelderlin, Schiller and Goethe still viewed the task of the poet as priestly, they barely were able to present a redeeming god and his normative beauty. Although Schiller restrains drama to such an immanent moral function, Hoelderlin shows some openness to the transcendent in his insistence that a poet's life must become a total commitment to an irresistable flooding of endless love in the mystery of worldly being. (A30 15, A36 656, 848ff)

In order to perceive and convey this splendor and love, the artist must, of course, possess a highly active sensitivity to form and the ability to create symbols. He must fuse the greatest moral beauty with the greatest sensible beauty in such a way that no concept can possibly do his creation justice. (A36 722) His idea must be plunged so profoundly into natural symbols that it can never be extricated and isolated from this bond. The bond allows the natural symbol with its given, necessary meaning to express a free idea that cannot be expressed in any other way. The viewer's access to this idea or meaning can be obtained solely by prolonged contemplation of the form that unites the various natural symbols.

Even more than other forms of knowledge and communication the knowledge and language of art require the presence of love. For Goethe love is the "painter of landscapes" and the origin of the art of poetry. (A36 703, 714) Love enables the poet to see and create the beautiful and thus no one can see the beautiful in an art work without the eyes of love. (A36 174) This necessity of love, however, is by no means peculiar to the language of art but simply especially obvious there.

This entire treatment of the spirituality of action has been concerned with the communication of love by love. Whether this communication occurs in the language of nature, of words or of art, its power of conviction lies in the love it communicates. The self, therefore, must be transparent to divine love and we have seen in the spiritualities of eros and activity the steps that man can undertake to achieve this transparency. His steps of desire and action are, however, always responses to the divine initiative and therefore must be rooted in his receptivity to the divine.

Chapter Four

THE SPIRITUALITY OF RECEPTIVITY

The role of receptivity in contemplation has been discussed but we must now consider the decisive role played by the readiness to surrender one's entire self into the hands of the divine. We must see how the readiness to enjoy the splendor of the Absolute implies the readiness to be possessed and used by it and thus to lose control painfully over one's own destiny. Because the aesthetic search for the supremely beautiful is so likely to produce an aesthete who flees all pain and for that very reason flees the transcendent, the spirituality of receptivity must be given central importance.

Primacy of Receptivity Over Eros

There is a danger in both the spirituality of eros and of action that they will not seriously face the question of the Absolute, of its otherness and transcendence. The spirituality of eros tends towards a naive theism in that it simply seeks "something" beyond the limited beings; the spirituality of action tends towards a naive atheism or agnosticism in that it simply has no time at the moment to pursue the question of the Absolute. In order, therefore, that the basic philosophical act of wonder be preserved, it is necessary that both of these spiritualities rise out of and merge into a spirituality of receptivity.

Balthasar calls it a spirituality of _Indifferenz_ and there is perhaps no word in his vocabulary that better expresses his understanding of man's basic disposition. (A36 242ff) He understands it fully in the light of Ignatius of Loyola's _indifferencia_ which means almost the exact opposite of the English word "indifference." It is _the_ religious virtue and closely affiliated with Vergil's understanding of _pietas_: the readiness at every moment and in every situation to hear and answer the word of the Absolute spoken in the word of Being. (A36 434, 467f, 382f) It includes above all courage, humility, awe, trust and prayer as directed towards the personal truth, goodness and splendor of the Absolute. It is described and portrayed clearly by Homer, the tragedians, and Vergil; by the Christian mystics and authors of "spiritual theology"; and by Hoelderlin and Heidegger. (A36 407ff, 776ff)

Above all it serves as a corrective to an understanding of human transcendence that sees desire and appetite as man's basic act. (A10 291ff, A28 63) The basic act must be selfless receptivity if the good and the true are to be sought only together with the beautiful. Receptivity sees the beauty of goodness and truth because it enjoys them for their own sake and not in order to fulfil a desire for self-enrichment. (A30 145, A31 138, A34 19ff) Plato, Plotinus (A36 26, 599) and Augustine (A36 969) all realized that the ascent of eros must climax not in the desire to possess and to use (_uti_) but in an enjoyment (_frui_) that is ready to be possessed and used. (A40 57) If the basic human act is seen as desire, it is all but inevitable that the subject will attempt to make use of his god, to impose limits on the god's freedom by defining beforehand what the god must do to fulfil man. The primary ethical commandment then becomes "Know thyself"; know your own nature and know what it needs to become authentic; obey a conscience that is rooted not in the other but in oneself; obey a categorical imperative that is not transcendent but transcendental. (A12 274) This is the philosophy of a masculine mind (B132 346, B58 43) that is determined to acquire and maintain strict control over its own fate, to be autonomous and to avoid risks and unforeseeable suffering. The highest human faculty in this philosophy and the means of transcendence is the will. (A36 859, 879) God is allowed at most to serve as a safeguard or guarantee of the human moral order but strictly denied any free will of his own or the power to place an unforeseeable demand on man. The light of such a god is readily identified with the light of reason or natural law and thus fully utilized.

This is the Titanic, Promethean tendency that Plato recognized as basic to all philosophy in its overcoming and enlightening of the world of myth. (A36 95, 143f) It is the rationale of a heart that is no longer willing "to suffer the slings and arrows of outrageous fortune" inflicted on man by the unforeseeable and incomprehensible decisions of the gods. For Homer, the tragedians, and Vergil the basic human virtue was not to acquire control over one's fate and fend off suffering either theoretically or practically but to patiently endure it. (A36 242, 52ff) Nothing is more characteristic of Odysseus, Aeneas and the tragic heroes than their humble receptivity to the gods' will. Human transcendence meant for them not the carefully controlled ascent of human reason and will to a perfect understanding and control over man's destiny (A40 266f) but being plunged into the humiliating and excruciating life of an exile in the polis of the gods. (A32 817) One transcended into the divine realm only by totally losing control over one's own fate and by becoming absolutely dependent on the mercy of one's fellow man and the gods. The distinction between God and man was too great that man could approach God by serenely contemplating the image of God within his soul. Transcendence meant being dragged and shoved out of one's own familiar world into a totally foreign world where one has no rights, no authority and no power. (A36 117) What the Greeks and Vergil thus describe as an exile or an odyssey is described by Plotinus as a desert, by the mystics as the dark night of the soul, and by Hoelderlin and Heidegger as the strange country. They all realize that the beginning and end of all knowledge and understanding is not power and control but weakness and obedience. They recognize the non-existence of an autonomous reason deciding on the basis of its own evidence whether or not it will make the irrational leap of faith. Rather reason realizes that it never was autonomous and never will be; it attributes its seemingly autonomous ability to know and measure objects to its already being known and measured by the Absolute. (A10 295ff, 45ff) Man's most natural act and the very birth of his reason lies in his obedience to the measure offered by the Absolute. (A30 434, A10 275)

Prayer and Expropriation

Because obedience presupposes a speaker and a respondent, intersubjectivity must be the central question of philosophy and prayer the only possible posture for objective knowledge. (A32 111f) Western philosophy has, however, replaced intersubjectivity at its center with theory and practice. It replaces the absolute subject with an impersonal object abstracted from the free, unpredictable, personal gods of the mythic world. Like all abstractions this one was necessary but a grave impoverishment. (A36 73) The abstraction is necessary in order that God not appear simply as another being but as Absolute Being and the Non-aliud. But by means of this abstraction God's sovereign freedom is denied and he becomes identified with natural law in the Stoa, the moral order for Fichte and human intersubjectivity for Feuerbach. Such a development eliminates from philosophy the possibility of dialogue with the Absolute. (A36 143f, 167ff) Those Stoics who recognized this development as a step not beyond but behind myth interpreted their philosophy in the light of myth and allowed it to issue in authentic prayer. (A36 252) This culmination in prayer is the criterion of true receptivity (A36 412) and proves the truth of Hoelderlin's piety inspite of his theoretical rejection of transcendence. (A36 654ff, 677) It is Eckhart who unintentionally prepares for the substitution of rational speculation for prayer in modern philosophy by focusing primarily on God's reason rather than his love and by seriously obscuring the distinction between man's reason and God's reason. (A36 405, 850f) Man's ultimate act is thus bound to become that of possessive gnosis instead of awestricken worship and love. Bruno is the first modern to see this substitution and to declare the impossibility of prayer. (A36 607) Shaftesbury equates it with enthusiasm (A36 640f) while Kant (836f) and Fichte (886ff) although trying to make room for some kind of worship and prayer make it impossible by their total denial of free will and personality in the Absolute. Goethe too cannot pass beyond his reverence for things to true prayer. (A36 694, 699, 735, 748) The inability to pray ultimately means the loss of Being, of love, and of meaning and thus the movement from metaphysical wonder to metaphysical science. (A36 973, 959)

If however, intersubjectivity and prayer are maintained, metaphysics will involve an expropriation of the subject by the Absolute and a sacrificial surrender of the self. The self-sacrifice for another human that crowns the spirituality of action must be grounded ultimately in a receptivity to the free will of the Absolute. The two figures of classical poetry that best represent this expropriation are probably Oedipus and Aeneas. The gods demonstrate their freedom to expropriate them both by stripping them of anything they could possibly offer as being worthy of honor and by plunging them into a life of humiliation and tragedy. (A36 123) All the defenses such as kinship, accomplishments, virtue and knowledge that the ego uses to place itself on a pedestal are ruthlessly torn down. (A36 115 f) All that formerly constituted their identity is torn from them so that they stand totally impoverished and naked before man and the gods. (A36 415f, 517ff, 434ff) By accepting this expropriation they sacrifice themselves in order to portray the true human situation: boundless dependence upon the Absolute. Both represent all mankind (A36 48, 95, A40 348) and Vergil in a special way the Romans. (A36 240ff) As representative of mankind, they demonstrate the inadequacy of all the other things man depends on for fulfilment: the love of a woman, the fidelity of friends, the glorification by the poets. They demonstrate the futility of trying to defend oneself against the pain of our tragic existence. (A36 104) They demonstrate the guilt from which man can never be extracted without a total uprooting of his existence. They and the humanity they represent experience the Absolute more and more in its absence so that their own pain becomes a medium of transcendence---a transcendence in the night. (A36 437, 117, 599, 467) The free acceptance of this pain in contradiction to all his desires for himself allows the hero to transcend his self into the divine realm. Suffering's destruction of man's illusions about himself and its revelation of man's true situation effects the ontological process that Aristotle describes as Catharsis. Man is purified and elevated out of his limited, self-centered view of existence. (A40 353ff) This limited self in its carefully ordered and well defended existence undergoes a sacrificial death in that it stretches and extends itself into the realm of the Absolute and begins to see existence in the light of the Absolute. (A31 138f) Its childhood vision of the horizon of Absolute Love is revived.

Receptivity as Activity

Although the renewed vision occurs in that the self is expropriated and sacrificed by the Absolute, such receptivity by no means implies a destruction of the creature's freedom. Even though man is not autonomous in the Kantian sense, nor is he heteronomous in the Kantian sense. (A24 79) All that was said in the description of the spirituality of action about free choice and free action is not surpassed but fulfilled in the spirituality of receptivity. Man never gives a merely passive acknowledgment to whatever the Absolute does for or with him but must actively await the action of the Absolute as the bride awaits her bridegroom; as the devoted servant, the command of his master; as the artist's hand, the dictate of his inspiration; and as the actor, the demands of his role. (A12 293) This receptivity is in its passivity the highest human activity.

The centrality of such active passivity has been emphasized by various authors. Euripides insists that glory radiates from Alcestes self-sacrifice for her husband only because she is feely and actively accepting the divine will. (A36 134) For the Zen Buddhist this active receptivity is man's co-operation with the Absolute and as such determines what the Absolute is capable of doing in and with man. (A30 564) Ignatius of Loyola provides the decisive correction to the quietistic tendencies in the mystics, Luther, the "spiritual writers" and the later Fichte. (A12 274, A36 455ff) Heidegger lays great stress on one's receptivity to Being as the pre-requisite for the dialogue within the "hermeneutical circle" where all understanding takes place. (A36 778) It is the ground of man's free activity and therefore of his very humanity. (A15 80ff, C16 41-46, A10 306ff, A36 399)

This free active receptivity to the initiative of the Absolute does not lead to an exclusive preoccupation with the Absolute but becomes the ground of man's activity in the world. The Absolute does not permit man to remain turned away from creatures but sends him to them and demands total absorption in this mission. Thus Fichte urges man to spend his entire life as one who has been sent while constantly looking back to the one who sent him. (A36 888) Every man must be as possessed by his mission as an actor is by his role. The actor becomes possessed by his role in that he places himself totally at its service yet remains vividly aware that he is not identical with the person he impersonates. He must struggle not to interfere with the presentation. The total engagement of his entire person in the service of the role should culminate not in identity with the role but in an endless, intensive dialogue with the role. The Absolute demands the same kind of engagement and likewise rejects a final identity. Like the Absolute the role demands of the actor that he forget everything extraneous to the role and serve it totally for its own sake. (B9 84f) The more the actor acts for the sake of his own fame, the less receptive he will be to the role and the more he will read himself into it. The major difference between a theatrical role and a real role is the difficulty in establishing what the real role is. The off-stage play is constantly being conceived, written and produced all at the same time. This forces the off-stage actor to continually struggle to know how his role will continue and end. (A27 31, D34 the postscript) Off-stage one must expect totally unexpectable and radical changes in ones role and be able to respond to them immediately. Greek tragedy showed a profound awareness of this analogy between a role on stage and a mission in life. The actors were originally priests and the divinity was believed to possess the actor and appear in him. The drama, therefore, was a sacrament and could be produced only for believers. (A36 99ff)

The Witness of Self-Sacrifice

If a man's life is as totally absorbed by his mission as an actor's by his role, his words and his deeds will achieve the same kind of unification and harmony. Every aspect of the self will have a specific part to play in the service of the other. His entire life will be a single, unified, proportioned self-sacrifice. Euripides' Alcestis (A36 132) and Hoelderlin's Death of Empedocles (A36 635) show clearly the necessity of self-sacrifice for the fulfillment of one's mission. Alcestis saves her husband and Empedocles, like every poet, stands with a naked, exposed heart ready to call down a blessing upon the earth through his death for others. Such dying for others fulfils the human mission to communicate the Absolute because it unites man most intimately to both the Absolute and the creaturely. His obedience to the Absolute and his solidarity with the creature make him most transparent to the Absolute and therefore the best mediator. His self-sacrifice radiates most vividly of all the splendor of Absolute Love to the beloved creature. The classical poets were keenly aware of the splendor that pours out of the man who is willing to die or actually dies for his people in obedience to the gods. The beauty of Homer's heroes is grounded in their free acceptance of death at the command of Zeus. Divine splendor shines through them precisely "in the misery of their mortality and in the horror of the death that threatens them from every side." (A36 51ff) Likewise Sophocles recognizes in man the divine image because of his willingness to accept death as the will of the gods. (A36 117) By accepting the death that the gods have decreed, Antigone and Oedipus render an external epiphany of the gods superfluous. (A36 139) "Their suffering at the moment of death radiates divine splendor from within." Above all the bruised, disfigured, humiliated body of Oedipus radiates a splendor that surpasses that of the most "beautiful" body and brings salvation first to Thebes and later to Athens. (A36 119ff, 47f) Such total impoverishment of the self and loss of human beauty makes room in the person for divine splendor to dwell and appear. Thus Socrates receives a whole new splendor from his sacrificial death. The same phenomenon can be seen in Vergil's Aeneas who totally subordinates himself to the mission of founding Rome and like Abraham ventures out into a totally strange land to surrender his life for the sake of his descendents. At the command of the gods he burns up his entire life for the Roman people. (A36 238-49) Vergil himself sacrificed his self for his people in that his exalted hopes in the Emperor and the future of Rome were brutally shattered during his own life and brought him laughter, scorn and humiliation. In addition he was shy, awkward and sickly. Yet precisely out of this humiliated, pathetic figure radiates such a splendor that he has been loved and revered for 2000 years as the father of Western culture. (A36 250) Marx, like Hesiod, points to self-sacrifice as the basic moment of man's economic, political and private life and as the source of human if not divine splendor. (A36 921ff, 77f) Heidegger in turn calls upon man to let his anxiety force him to relinguish his control over reality and thus venture out of his self into an "unknown country." He must open himself to the realm of Being that can be neither grasped in a concept nor controlled by law, wealth or technology.

All of these witnesses have pointed to the moment of self-sacrifice as the primary point of mediation between the splendor of the Absolute and the heart of man. Because of his transparency the man who sacrifices himself is recognized as the supreme source of salvation for his people. His sacrifice is salvific because it enables those who see it to believe once again in a horizon of Absolute Love. The Absolute like all other lovers proves that He is love ultimately only by demonstrating His willingness to take upon Himself the suffering of His beloved. He must show Himself like Zeus in the Illiad greatly burdened by the Trojan war and weeping in his indecision about whom to help and whom to hinder. (A36 65f) The Absolute can show His solidarity by inflicting suffering on someone with whom He is united in an especially intimate relation. The man who is so enraptured by the Absolute that he is willing to leave behind everything else and even his own life proves that he has entered such a relation with the divine. If this man then, inspired by his god, takes upon himself the agony of his people, he proves that the Absolute itself is willing to assume this agony. Being able to do this he will be able to turn his people around, to re-volutionize them. By opening to them the horizon of Absolute Love he offers them the greatest possiblity of self-transcendence.

Celebration

Self-sacrifice, therefore, can be seen as the culmination of all three spiritualities. The erotic ascent constantly demands that one leave his old self behind. Action that seeks to further the self-communicating Absolute Love requires the proof of self-sacrifice for its credibility. Receptivity that results in possession by the Absolute presupposes and effects an emptying or dying of the self that makes room for the possessor. Although the reality of the pain involved in such self-sacrifice is not to be denied much more important is the joyous response to the Absolute Splendor that grounds the necessity of self-sacrifice. Man's abiding, fundamental response to the grace of divine beauty is thanksgiving and joyous celebration. Even though his receptivity to the Absolute does mean being led out into a strange land, such exile is effected by a delightful, delicate, enrapturing beauty. (A10 254, A36 66) The receptive man receives Being as a friendly, intimate home and hearth, a joyous song and a festival that must be celebrated in the insane turbulance of Carneval. (A36 723ff, 756ff)

The classical poets expressed this enchanting aspect of Being with the word **charis**, which is perhaps best approximated by our word "gracefulness." Pindar uses the term frequently and applies it to the radiance of a victorious athlete. He describes it as follows: "It is the loving fusion of the victor's dignity and the poet's praise... Charis is everything that causes joy, both the joy given and the joy received. It is the giving itself as well as the gift and the gift's value.... . The divine Charites dip existence into the golden light of charm and joy without which life would not be worth living.... . They permit the meaning of existence to reveal itself as a relationship of love that causes and is constituted by joy." (A36 91) This gracefulness evokes the pleasure that for Thomas constitutes the very definition of beauty; id quod visum placet, that which pleases when it is seen. It also causes Augustine to designate the basic human disposition towards the transcendent as enjoyment, frui, rather than use, uti. (A32 134)

Like eros and action this enjoying receptivity is basicly other-directed and thus consists primarily in thanksgiving and celebration. Because of one's joy, he feels himself subjected to a new categorical imperative: "Act as if you, your fellow man and all things owed thanks to a groundless grace for your existence." (A36 963) The central importance of this thanksgiving for a fullness of understanding appears in the great weight Heidegger places on the common etymology of "thinking" and "thanking." (A36 777) True thanksgiving, according to Fichte, is a surrendering of oneself back into the love out of which ones existence arose and thus the common link that unites eros, action and receptivity. (A37 887) The unifying act of thanksgiving receives its highest expression in praise which thereby becomes the primary task of the thinker as well as the poet. (A36 661, 763, 769)

Conclusion

Part One has dealt with the philosophical attempt to understand the splendor of Absolute Being and has described the necessity of contemplation, erotic desire, action and receptivity. All of these movements are elements of the metaphysical wonder which is the only disposition capable of perceiving the splendor of the Absolute. It now appears that this wonder finds its culmination in celebration. At the heart of philosophical method lies the aesthetic act of celebration. The object of this celebration is the horizon of Absolute Love and, therefore, the basic question for all philosophy is whether it can find, in the face of all the forces of non-love, sufficient evidence to maintain its vision of this horizon. Or does the maintenance of this vision require new evidence that is provided solely by the splendor of Christ's form?

Part II

THE SPLENDOR OF CHRIST IN THEOLOGICAL METHOD

Part Two will show that a basic task of theology is to make the splendor of Christ appear in such a way that even in the face of death man's experience of the ultimate horizon as love is radically deepened and confirmed. At the heart of theological method lies the aesthetic task of helping the splendor of Christ to appear to all men, to continually crucify men's aesthetic sensitivities and to awaken them to the fullest possible act of wonder and celebration. By doing this theology accomplishes the supreme aesthetic achievement of mainting the paradoxical unity of continuity in discontinuity, of life in death, of form in formlessness, of glorification in crucifixion. The theologian is then able to demand the death of philosophical aesthetics and to portray the unexpectable uniqueness of Christ's form without being driven to the extremes of annihilating the lasting, inherent dignity of the created form or of reducing Christ's splendor to fit the creature's expectations and needs.

Chapter One on the theological a priori discusses the Christological ground of creation and therefore of philosophy and science. Such a ground establishes a continuity between philosophical and theological aesthetics in opposition to the positivism of dialectical theology. A vision of this continuity, however, has continually misled theologians to an a priorism wherein any distinction between philosophy and theology is lost. Such a priorism undervalues the uniqueness of Christ's a posteriori evidence, which will be discussed in a second chapter. It will attempt to show that Christ's form can be presented as the most splendid form conceivable and yet not one that man could construct. The third chapter will dwell on the theologian's dependence on his own a posteriori subjective evidence. Without the experience of conformation to Christ's cross and a felt sharing in his resurrection, the theologian could not verify Christianity. The concluding chapter will deal with the theologian's resulting witness to all men and his responsiblity to maintain the purity of the church's witness.

Chapter One

THE THEOLOGICAL A PRIORI

Its Proper Role

The question to be answered in this chapter is why there are the anticipations of the Christian vision that were pointed out in Part One. The theologian's response to this question should be to show that Christ is the beginning and the end of the universe. (1Cor 8:6; Col 1:16f; Apoc 2:8, 3:14) The guidelines for doing this will be provided in this chapter and thereby the continuity between philosophical and theological aesthetics will be grounded.

To say that Christ is the beginning and the end of the universe means that not only does Christ exist in the universe but even more so the universe exists in him; he does not exist to save the world but the world exists to be saved by him. Thus a supernatural destiny grounds all created nature. The Father created all things in Christ's image so that they could ultimately become part of his imagery of the Father. (A14 297f, 337ff, A27 51) Christ, therefore, is the measure of man, so that man's destination for union with Christ belongs to a proper definition of his concrete historical existence. (A14 357, A32 609f) Yet even though Christ is the exemplary and final cause of man, this origin and destiny is not natural but supernatural. No one has a right to it even though no one exists without it. It is a theological a priori that does not constitute man's humanity but is a freely given modification of the religious a priori he possesses as a created human being.

His religious a priori is the ability to know God that was described in Part I. It is given to man when he is made a subject. He becomes a knowing, measuring subject only because he is known and measured by the divine subject and thereby given the ability to know his measurer. (A30 31, 237, 433; A21 33f) (4) Both Ebeling and Balthasar strongly emphasize this origin of humanity in God's knowledge, idea and word. God is man's basic situation, his beginning and end, the mystery of reality revealed in the basic word of reality. (W&G II 27, 57ff, 83) (5) The divine origin of subjectivity can be expressed as participation of the light of the mind in the light of Being and thereby in the light of the Absolute. (A30 158, A36 568) It means that the divine light is present in the depths of man's natural subjectivity; that God is more interior than man's own interiority; that he is the inner teacher. (A32 308) God's light is the transcendental presupposition of all rationality and all knowledge, the light in which man sees the light. (A32 111f, 310, 236, 630, A28 23ff)

This religious a priori is radically broadened and transformed by the theological a priori. It perceives a new word beyond the word of creation, and a new light beyond the light of Being. (A30 155, 274, A32 113) (6) A new act of God occurs. Just as man's religious a priori is rooted in God's love and understanding, so too his theological a priori is derived from God's new understanding and love for him. (A30 316f) The Father knows and loves him "in Christ," measures him with the form of Christ and gives him a participation in Christ's knowledge and love. Thus God's word and his new light reveal his own interior life, the life of the Trinity. The light of man's intellect acquires a new participation in the inner light of God and becomes the light of faith. This light alone enables man to see the inner life of God in Christ's

(4) Ebeling, Gerhard, Wort und Glaube II, Tuebingen 1969, p. 57; abbreviated in the text as W&G II

(5) Ebeling, Gerhard, Gott und Wort, Tuebingen 1966, p. 83ff, 54ff, Eng. trans. God and Word, Fortress Press 1967; abbreviated in text as G&W

(6) Fuchs, Ernst, Marbuerger Hermeneutik, Tuebingen 1968, p. 244; abbreviated in text as Fuchs M.H.

form, to hear and answer his call. (A40 35, A30 156) God's knowing and grasping man anew gives man a new certitude and a new evidence. (A30 126) Man does not reach out to grasp the new light, but the light enters or is "infused" into his depths; it grasps him and draws him out beyond himself. The divine <u>agere</u> preceeds the new <u>esse</u> and establishes a new ontological ground for man's new cognition. (A32 505, A14 375) Before man begins to act, to know and to love, the Spirit has poured into him the deed that God has already done for him. (A40 241) This deed is the death and resurrection of Christ which becomes the theological a priori in Christians and non-Christians. It becomes God's interior witness to the external form of Christ. (A30 149)

Saying that the theological a priori presupposes the religious a priori means that this new light and new word encounter and transform man at the point where he intuits the absence of Absolute Being in contingent Being and where he constructs his myths. (A30 137, A32 308f, 113, A40 37) Because the new word emerges out of the mystery of Being as its ultimate ground, it arises in man as a new light out of the light of his intellect. (A30 151ff) The light of reason in its concrete existence, therefore, is imbedded in supernatural faith. (A14 361) The receptivity, openness and eros before the total horizon of Being constitute man's very subjectivity and provide the womb which the seed of divine love enters and fructifies. The new seed enables the subject to bear totally new fruits, gives it a new openness to a new horizon, a new realm in which to exercise its human freedom. (A32 746, 628f) The light of the Trinity, because it is transpersonal, becomes a new transcendental of all human knowledge making the redeemer as intimately present in the depths of man's heart as the creator. (A40 37, A32 113) A new dynamic energy is poured out into the most human in man giving a new form to his mind and a new strength to his will. A new weight, the <u>pondus amoris</u>, becomes a new source of life within man driving him out beyond his natural capacity. (A30 105) The supernatural, the promise of salvation and the desire for it, is written into his natural foundation. (B18 94, A40 19) Therefore the openness and dynamism of man's created nature finds its completely undeserved and unexpectable yet in every way proper fulfillment in its new supernatural destiny. (A14 355, B69 460) Catholic theology's emphasis on this preservation and reverence for created nature in the act of redemption (<u>gratia non destruit</u>) enables the theologian to show the newness and radicalness of the transformation that grace brings (<u>sed extollit naturam</u>). (A14 378)

Because this new light is the light of the Trinity, it draws man out into a participation in the inmost life and light of God. His participation in the very nature of God effects a connaturality between God and man. (A40 241) This ontological participation is necessary if there is to be any personal cognitive interchange between God and man. Just as inter-human communication is made possible only by men's communion in a common nature so too there must be some commonness of nature to allow communication between God and man. If God's nature were <u>totally</u> other than man's, there could be no communication between them. (A40 32ff) With all preservation of the "greater dissimilarity" between God and man, there must be a certain analogy even between man's created nature and God's, but this similarity is deepened by grace to an "incredible" intimacy and even familiarity. (A40 37ff) Without this communication of Being God could not possibly communicate his truth, for

God's truth and his Being are inseparable. In that he does draw man's entire humanity into the sphere of the Trinity, God turns man's mind, self-consciousness and love into an image of the Trinity. (A30 174, A32 235) Man participates in God's omnipotence and a new proportionality arises between divine and human power. (7) Because only God can know God, it is solely this proportionality that enables man to see the Trinity in Christ. (B130 12) It gives man a new inclination and readiness to receive the exterior revelation of the Trinity vaguely in all beings and supremely in Christ. (A30 439ff)

This interior witness of the Father is mediated by Christ, merited by him and fully directed towards enabling us to receive him. The divine presence in the light of faith is the presence of the Spirit who is there solely to reveal the love between Christ and the Father. As the "we" between the Father and Christ and, therefore, between the Father and all mankind, the Spirit provides the non-objective, a priori light that enables us to see the Trinitarian light in Christ. (A40 101, A34 49) As the love between the Father and the Son, he gives us the love to answer the Trinitarian love in Christ. He turns the human situation into a kerygmatic situation, i.e. a situation in which man is able to understand the Christological kerygma in its necessity. (T&V 51) He gives man Mary's eager readiness to affirm a priori whatever is to be revealed in Christ no matter what the consequences. (A40 163, 240, A39 31f) He begins to eliminate from man all the preconditions about what revelation can or must mean and enables man to place himself entirely at Christ's disposal. (B18 94, A30 493f) He opens up a new horizon and a new future by enabling the believer to recognize and unify all aspects of Christ into a form that reveals the Trinity. (A40 38) The divine light in Christ's form convinces the believer because the believer already has the initial rays of divine light within him. (A30 155) The weight of love within him draws him to the unique beauty of Christ.

Because the Father has chosen all men from eternity to participate in his love, they all have this sensitivity to the light of the Trinity. (A30 151) All minds are illumined by the light of faith and placed in an inner relation to the a posteriori light of revelation. (A30 160) Because all men participate in the supernatural goal of humanity and thus in the means to achieve it, pure nature and pure reason are non-existent abstractions. (A14 209, 299, 335) Thus any contemplation of Being that would attempt to be "purely" philosophical or purely natural would be unfaithful to itself. (A14 357) Vague anticipation of Trinitarian Love can be found in most philosophies and religions. (A30 160f, 149ff, A31 306) For this reason explicit knowledge of the Trinity in Christ is experienced as a returning to one's primal intuitions. (A14 272)

---

(7) Ebeling, Gerhard, Theologie und Verkündigung, Tuebingen, 1963, p. 15; Eng. trans. Theology and Proclamation, Fortress Press 1966, abbreviated in text as T&V.

A Priorism

Once the theological a priori has been recognized and thus Christ's power to fulfil man seen to be operative in all men, the crucial question is an aesthetic one: what role is played by the encounter with Christ's objective form in history? How important is it for the theologian to be able to make visible the splendor of Christ by demonstrating the inner-necessity and harmony of his form? How dependent is Christian faith on such a vision? Can a believer maintain his metaphysical wonder before Absolute Love on the evidence of the theological a priori or is he necessarily dependent on the evidence of Christ's objective form? The underlying thesis of Balthasar's theological aesthetics is that in the face of death it is impossible for anyone consistently to maintain a belief in Absolute Love, unless he sees the splendor of Christ's form. The a posteriori vision, therefore, is of primary importance.

As a central figure in the "new quest for the historical Jesus" Ebeling is in close agreement with Balthasar and has criticized Barth and Bultmann for basically the same reasons as Balthasar. Balthasar, however, refers to Ebeling only once (A40 86) and still finds him like Barth and Bultmann and Rahner insufficiently critical of his Kantian presuppositions. They all tend to overvalue the a priori and undervalue the a posteriori.

Part One was basically a discussion of Balthasar's response to the philosophical a priorism of which Kant is the most influential exponent. Just as the main characteristic of that philosophical tradition was its implacable tendency to monism, so too its effect on theology is a monism of faith. When Kant declares pure reason to be a "factory of idols" when it attempts to know the infinite and when he then restricts the knowledge of God to the practical reason's a priori awareness of the categorical imperative, he removes the human spirit from the limits of time and space and places it in direct contact with the divine. The finite object ceases to play any role in the knowledge of the infinite. The inevitable tendency of such a position is to trivialize man's knowledge of finite forms and to define man almost entirely in terms of his desire for and knowledge of the infinite. For theologians this tends to mean that man is faith, that grace is his being and not a mode of his nature. Man all but has no finite senses and finite reason but is by his very nature pure communion with the infinite.

In the dialectical theology of Barth and Bultmann this is translated to mean that the human is totally other than the divine and sundered from it by an unbridgeable chasm. Following Luther's lead they come perilously close to identifying the human with the sinful and declaring it incapable of having anything to do with the divine. They almost go to the extreme of designating creation as non-being and the divine as being. With time, however, both have gradually moved towards some kind of analogy between divine and human being. Although Bultmann has recently admitted that perhaps the later Heidegger has provided some kind of formal knowledge of God, neither Barth nor Bultmann are willing to admit that man can progress from a knowledge of the created to a knowledge of the uncreated except through "the Word." (8) Bultmann interprets the Word as a trans-historical, invisible call to the individual for decision. Barth denies that any analogy is visible to the non-Christian between the Word and any other word. For Bultmann, therefore, the knowledge of God remains unrelated to the knowledge of temporal and spatial forms and for Barth God can be perceived in forms only by one who has explicitly confessed the divinity of Christ. (A30 370) Ultimately, however, this knowledge of Christ's form is superfluous for Barth because all men are saved whether they know it or want it by the Father's trans-historical decision to save them. Neither Barth nor Bultmann, therefore, are willing to rely on man's aesthetic sensitivity for ultimate fulfillment.

Barth relies purely on an a priori divine action and Bultmann, Rahner and Ebeling all rely very heavily on some variation of the a priori categorical imperative. They tend to view the human as a void seeking to be filled by the supernatural knowledge of God. Although Rahner insists that man has a nature with its own proper fulfillment in a natural knowledge of God, he lays such great emphasis on the "supernatural existential" as man's a priori, erotic pursuit of a supernatural knowledge of God, that it is difficult to take man's nature with any seriousness. (A14 311f) A hypothetical nature without grace would seem to be almost nothing but need, despair, emptiness and even nothingness. For the Lutherans Bultmann and Ebeling, to be human tends to mean almost exclusively standing before the hidden God who convinces man of his own nothingness.

The only goodness in the universe and, therefore, the only Being seems to be some variation of the categorical imperative: grace or faith or God's knowledge of himself as it occurs in a state of multiplicity. (A14 217ff, A36 331f) As in the neo-Platonic tradition man seems to be God striving to return from a state of multiplicity to a state of unity. All three theologians would, of course, vigorously deny this interpretation of their thought but their acceptance of Kantian presuppositions compels them irresistibly in this direction. The only thing of significance in man is his longing for salvation, for freedom, for authenticity, and this longing is grounded in the divine spark that constitutes his Being. His experience of the world tells him he is nothing, but the divine spark within tells him to pursue the infinite. This divine spark has a mystical origin as can be seen in Marechal's designation of it as a mystical experience of identity and a feeling of presence. (A14 303ff) Marechal, Rahner, Ebeling and Bultmann all tend to follow Kant in making this a priori knowledge the ultimate criterion for the knowledge of God. (A40 83ff)

Verification Through Reduction

Therefore, the truth that Christ reveals tends very strongly to derive its credibility less and less from the splendor of his form and more and more from its

---

(8) Bultmann, Rudolf, Glauben und Verstehen IV, Tuebingen 1964 p. 106

ability to fulfil man's a priori need and expectation. The Lutheran tradition finds itself expressed in Melanchton's words, "To know Christ is to know what Christ does for us."(9) The Lutheran rejection of any "speculative" theology means that Christ and God can be known only from the soteriological perspective as he who fulfils man's needs. God, therefore, can be known only as Nicholas of Cues knows him, as the "reconciliation of opposites." The danger inherent in this overemphasis on soteriology is that man sets about trying to understand the oppositions and tensions that cause his need, to decide how those oppositions can best be reconciled and to worship that reconciliation as his God.

To the extent that this happens, Jesus will tend to be accepted or rejected as a savior according to how well he fulfils one's expectations. A strong emphasis as in Ebeling's early theology on a theology of need makes it incumbent on the theologian to demonstrate how the encounter with the word of Christ gives man a continuous development and fulfillment of his self-understanding. The a posteriori encounter with Christ's form does not bring any blinding new evidence but tells man what he already wants and needs to hear by virtue of his "supernatural existential." In Rahner's words, "The external message of faith does not mediate the a posteriori motive of faith but mediates the a priori motive of faith to immediacy with itself."(10) Man has within him the evidence by which to verify Christ. He is not seriously dependent on Christ's form for the evidence it provides because the evidence of the a priori light of faith is identical with the evidence of Christ's form in history. "The logic of faith is not that which is learned categorically from outside but (exactly like natural logic in its initial act) the inner ontological structure of the act of faith itself."(11) The external revelation is the "categorical amplification of a transcendental piety," (A39 94) and it must be demythologized into its transcendental formality. (12) Even though Rahner tries to counteract this movement "over and over again" and to insist that transcendental revelation is mediated historically and not through non-historical introspection and mysticism, he still seems to severely denigrate all contemplation of the infinite in the finite by defining all knowledge of the finite as categorical. (13) As long as this Kantian terminology is used, the tendency is always near to interpret Jesus as a sign and an occasion that allows the transcendental relation to God to come to itself. The importance of the historical Christ of the synoptic gospels is badly neglected for the sake of the Johannine and Pauline Alpha and Omega. The Palestinian preacher is almost forgotten in the intense, exhaustive attention to the "supernatural existential" into which the Spirit has transformed him. Rahner is aware of this danger and strives to avoid it, but not to Balthasar's satisfaction. Balthasar finds it too hard to appreciate his distinction between the "anonymous Christian" with implicit faith and the explicitly confessing Christian. (A39 85ff)

(9) Bultmann, Ibid vol I 262, 267, vol II 154

(10) Rahner, Karl, Offenbarung und Ueberlieferung, Freiburg 1965 p. 23f

(11) Ibid p. 23

(12) Ibid p. 19

(13) Ibid p. 13f

The same tendency is even more pronounced in Bultmann and it is primarily in opposition to him that Balthasar wrote his theological aesthetics. (A30 302ff) In reaction to the historicists' attempt to construct an objective, factual account of Jesus' life as a basis for faith, Bultmann followed the Lutheran-Pietist-Kantian rejection of any kind of objectivity or speculation in religion. He followed the Kantian distinction between the categorical knowledge of being by pure reason and transcendent knowledge of infinite value by practical reason. (A36 829f) Thus he abandons to scientific reasoning the realm of history while locating religion entirely in the individual's decision in response to an eschatological call. History is the realm in which man attempts an aesthetic contemplation of the form of the Palestinian preacher, whereas the eschatological is the trans-historical, formless, invisible realm in which the individual decides to accept the "word" of Christ. The believer has to transcend visible forms offered as objects of faith because they are objectifications of interior experiences of the eschatological. They are of value only insofar as they mediate the self-understanding whence they came. Thus like Rahner Bultmann is interested in knowing the self-understanding or faith of John and Paul but emphasizes the illegitimacy of considering any "objective facts" that the synoptics offer.(14) To the extent that any author in the New Testament or the history of theology tries to present a visible form of Christ to be believed in, he is indulging in mythologization, i.e. the pre-modern belief that the finite is capable of revealing the infinite.(15) He is developing an aesthetic theology that must be demythologized. He must recognize the importance of Paul's faith being based on the fact that Jesus existed but he cannot and should not seek to know the form of Jesus. Modern man can and should not know God objectively but only non-objectively, i.e. as the condition for the possibility of man's self-understanding as one who has been forgiven. The evidence for his faith lies entirely in this subjective experience of forgiveness and not at all in the objective splendor of Christ's form.

Ebeling is known as a Bultmann disciple but he has made some very basic criticisms of his master that are similar to those made by Balthasar. These similarities will be discussed in the next chapter and we will examine here the basic affinity that still remains between master and disciple. Like Kant, Rahner and Bultmann, Ebeling sees man almost exclusively as need and desire whereas he sees God as the condition for the possibility of man's fulfillment. Man experiences the word of reality as the "law" and the most important effect of the law is to "hold man in the turbulence of his self-contradiction." (G&W 90) The law is "annihilating" temptation and the cause of despair that convinces man of his inability to be responsible to himself, his fellow man and to God. (W&G II 24, 38, 68) The experience of despair

(14) Bultmann, Rudolf, Theology of the New Testament, London 1952, pp. 577-81

(15) Bultmann, Rudolf, "Neues Testament und Mythologie," in Bartsch, Kerygma und Mythos I, Hamburg 1948, p. 22f

grounds the necessity and verification of the gospel. The need and desire to speak of God at all and to listen to the message of Christ are rooted in man's despair. (W&G II 293) Belief in God, therefore, is defined as expecting something from him and any attempt to know him other than as a saving power is to indulge in sinful objectifying speculation. (W&G II 310) This position leads Ebeling to such statements about theology as: "What continually guides theological thought in its hermeneutical task is the need of conscience." "Theology must remain a theology of need." (T&V 82, W&G II 295f)(16) "The basic structure and inner logic of Christianity is the gospel's overcoming the despair caused by the law."(17) Christianity, therefore, is true because it offers man what he desires: peace, certitude, freedom and the ability to love his brother. (W&G II 83, 245, 252ff, 370) God verifies himself by "verifying" man. (W&G II 32, 58, 345) The justification for this relying on need as a criterion of revelation is once again an a priorism. The a priori need is the primary source of all understanding and thus must be allowed a primary role in shaping the meaning of Christ's form.

Although this a priorism is nothing more than a tendency in all of these theologians and they are all aware of its dangers, Balthasar is still greatly mistrustful. Their acceptance of Kantian epistemology has not yet been so uncritical that it has led them to the ontological monism of the Idealists but they are dangerously close to being compelled against their wills to that extreme. (A39 58ff) He summarizes his fear in the term "Anthropological Reduction" by which he means the replacement of trusting belief in the free, Absolute Love of the incomprehensible Trinity by man's absolute knowledge of himself. (A34 19ff) It is the specter of Hegel that looms behind Barth, Bultmann, Rahner, Ebeling and Teilhard de Chardin as well. He foresees the frequent identification of the love of God and the love of man leading to an identification of God and man. If God is to be known only as a condition for the possibility of human fulfillment and if man's faith is to be identified with God's revelation, how far can we be from Hegel's monism? If man's humiliating reliance on the finite form becomes increasingly irrelevant, as the immediate access to the incomprehensible infinite is emphasized almost exclusively, what is to prevent man from thinking his knowledge to be absolute? If the evidence of the believer is the same as the evidence of the believed and if the transcendental structure of the believer determines the transcendental structure of the believed, what distinguishes them?(18) In order to prevent such Idealist conclusions from being drawn again, Balthasar, by means of his theological aesthetics, seeks to keep man mindful of his dependence on the finite form and therefore mindful of his own finitude. He continually emphasizes the importance of a posteriori, objective evidence.

---

(16) Ebeling, Gerhard, Luther, Eine Einfuehrung in sein Denken, p. 295 Tuebingen 1964, Eng. trans. Luther, An Intoduction to his Thought, Fortress Press 1970
(17) Ebeling, "Erwaegungen zu einer evangelischen Fundamentaltheologie" in Zeitschrift fuer Theologie und Kirche, 69, 1970 pp. 516ff
(18) Rahner, Karl, Schriften zur Theologie VIII, Einsiedeln p. 50f

Chapter Two

THE THEOLOGICAL A POSTERIORI

<u>The Agreement of Ebeling and Balthasar</u>

Balthasar's renewed emphasis on the a posteriori evidence of Christ's form begins in the metaphysics outlined in Part One. There it was obvious that he interprets man's fundamental disposition towards Being not as one of need and desire but one of receptive wonder. Therefore, when man approaches the gospel, he need not view himself as non-being longing for the grace of God to give him his very humanity but understands himself as a being capable of wonder, love and delight in the mystery of Being. Jesus, therefore, can verify himself not primarily by fulfilling man's need but by showing himself to be the most wondrous being conceivable.

Although Ebeling speaks of man's experience of reality outside of faith almost exclusively as an experience of law that leads him to despair, there are several passages in his writings where he begins to open the way to a new understanding of law. He points to the basic philosophic experience as reverence for the uncontrolable in the mystery of reality. This mystery infuses him with trust and allows him to show trust; it gives him the courage to love and to hope. (W&G II 207) The mystery fills him with shyness, piety, wonder and thankfulness; it penetrates to the center of his being: his receptivity as a meditative thinker. (W&G II 200) This receptivity is the ground of all philosophical theology and religion; the basis of faith is not what man does or makes but what happens to him and what he encounters. (W&G II 201) Thus man's most basic disposition towards reality is that of faith, hope and love. (G&W 47) In seeking to verify the unique Christian revelation, therefore, Ebeling refuses to follow the frequent theological route of denigrating non-Christian love. (19)

Recognizing with Balthasar the primacy of a theology of man as recipient over man as maker, Ebeling is led to a different understanding of language than Bultmann. A word is not primarily the objectification of a self-understanding and, therefore, a sign pointing away from itself, but comes very close to what Balthasar understands as form. (G&W 36ff) Under the influence of the later Heidegger, Ebeling along with Fuchs and Kaesemann view the word as the arrival and appearance of the mystery of Being. The mystery of Being is the original word of Being, the word of love that appears as hidden in all words. (W&G II 229)(20) It is the hidden that appears in

---

(19) Ebeling, Gerhard, <u>Einfuehrung in die theologische Sprachlehre</u>, Tuebingen 1971 p. 245

(20) Fuchs, Ernst, <u>Marburger Hermeneutik</u>, p. 244
<u>Gesammelte Aufsaetze III</u>, Tuebingen 1965 p. 308
Robinson, James, <u>Die Neue Hermeneutik</u>, Zuerich, 1965, p. 21, 71
Ebeling, <u>Theologische Sprachlehre</u>, p. 114

what can be grasped, not beside it but sacramentally, "in, with and under it."(21)
He warns against a superficial distinction between form and content and maintains
that a particular content can be revealed only in a particular form. (W&G II 111)(22)
Unlike Bultmann, therefore, he can speak of a language of the body and gesture and
insist on the inseparability of word and deed, of word and its situation. (W&G II 182,
29f; G&W 40f)(23) The words of nature, art, and action are not merely secondary
formulations or objectifications of an interior experience or self-understanding; they
are not a weakening of a greater reality "within" through a projection of it onto the
material world "outside." On the contrary man's reality is his love and his freedom
which he receives in every word he "hears" and realizes in every word he "speaks".
Ebeling's insistence, therefore, on the importance of "hearing" a word has much in
common with Balthasar's insistence on "seeing" a form.

Ebeling is well aware of the importance of a particular form for the particular
faith of Christians. With his profound Lutheran awareness of the power of law as the
power of death to rob man of his language and compel him to despair, Ebeling and
Balthasar agree on the ultimate inadequacy of all forms but one to keep open the
horizon of Absolute Love.

The Necessity of a Posteriori Evidence

Although Balthasar insists that it is not ultimately by virtue of Christ's ability to fulfil man's basic need that he is verified, he does dwell on the need created by
death as one reason man looks for new a posteriori evidence. Death reveals the inadequacy of philosophy, religion and the theological a priori for the maintenance of
wonder. In the face of death man refuses to rely on his aesthetic experiences of the
infinite in the finite, but relies more on his a priori evidence and is thereby led to a
monism and loss of wonder.

Death becomes such an acute problem to man because it is his nature to
transcend his nature and become a unique person. His human ego is awakened by a
thou and he comes to know himself as dependent on some kind of eternal thou. (A40
13ff) For this reason he comes to know with Euripides that the only true lover is one
who loves eternally. (A36 117, A45 10) Thus he can find ultimate human fulfillment
only by entering unique eternal relationships and coming to experience eternal love
in all dimensions of his life: the political and economic as well as the private. (A33
64ff) He is called to unite all of his unique personal relationships in one eternal personal relationship.

---

(21) Ebeling, Ibid. 246
(22) Ebeling, <u>Wort und Glaube I</u>, Tuebingen 1965 p. 24 abbreviated in text as W&G I
     Eng. trans. <u>Word and Faith</u>, Fortress Press 1963
(23) Ebeling, <u>Theologische Sprachlehre</u>, p. 95, 119ff

But how can he possibly continue to believe in an eternal thou who calls him to promise eternal love to a human thou if death means the destruction of his and his beloved's uniqueness? (A47 134ff) Why should he commit himself unconditionally to another and make the meaning of his life dependent on her love if this love has no unique, eternal significance? How can he love if Being is experienced not as an expression of eternal love, but as an ominous threat to the unique person, a threat that robs all man's unique personal activities of an ultimate meaning? (A36 958) He may find partial, temporary meanings for aspects of his life but death prevents him from finding any ultimate, total meaning for the whole of his existence. (A36 122ff, A47 129, A45 39f, A41 310) But if the whole of existence is ultimately meaningless, then every aspect of human activity is ultimately meaningless. (A33 67) Taking the enormous risks, suffering and sacrifices involved in committing oneself totally to another human being is definitely ridiculous.

The compulsion in the face of death to close in on oneself and to cease loving and wondering at the truth, goodness and beauty of Being is extremely strong in man. (A31 194) The suffering demanded of all true lovers is so great that they must be convinced of its ultimate meaning in order to keep from becoming more and more cautious in their love and building more and more impenetrable barricades around their all too defenseless human hearts. (A34 44) They are driven further and further back into their own private worlds of fantasy which are then sundered from the external world and carefully organized to guarantee their own security. (A20 131) They seal themselves off hermetically and will brutally exterminate any lover who tries to invade their private world. (A36 962, A32 6) This apparent self-love soon turns into self-hatred when they discover the guilt that penetrates their being from its very origins. They become aware of Kant's "radical evil" and Pascal's "second nature" which dominate man's nature before the exercise of his freedom and cannot be eliminated. (A31 200, A36 834, 781, A33 71, B93 299) Human freedom is the origin of all evil and was given to him by his creator. (A32 623, A6 50, A20 203) Thus only God as the giver of damning freedom can place man in a new situation where he can consistently know the true, choose the good and love the beautiful. Only if he has clear evidence that God can and wants to place him in this new situation, can he keep from closing himself off and falling deeper and deeper into despair. (A33 70) Without this evidence he must constantly distract himself to keep from noticing the boredom, superficiality, loneliness, hypocrisy and sadness that dominate his private world of fantasy. (A32 575, A20 340ff) The social conventions established in this world of more or less isolated subjects will make him increasingly immune to the injustice suffered by others. Stiffness and paralysis will cripple him and make the effort to love all but impossible. (A33 70) The greater the resulting indifference to the world around him becomes, the uglier the world appears. Hopkins bemoaned the ugliness of the industrial cities of England because it made Being less and less transparent to eternal love and plunged man deeper into his egotism. (A32 729) As Peguy bemoaned in the poor of France, such indifference plunges the destitute into an endless misery, a hell without hope. (A32 812f)

Hell is total isolation and solitude in which man is unable to communicate and thus unable to act humanly: he is turned into stone. (A20 338) He is filled with emptiness and feels himself increasingly subject to the suction of the abyss of nothingness. His person is devoured by meaninglessness and absurdity, and becomes a function of the chaos. (A20 342ff) All love having been stifled, he can attempt to understand the universe at best as a creation of reason or justice. Yet a God who creates such a universe in which man is damned to freedom and guilt must be rejected and cursed, as continually happens in contemporary literature, art and music. (A20 202, A24 174ff) Greek tragedy, inspite of its heroic efforts to justify the gods, finally rejects them as unjust. (A36 127ff) Israel because it, like all other religions and philosophies, is unable to free man of guilt and death, constantly places God's justice in question until Job, Coheleth and the apocalyptic writers finally declare earthly life so vain and meaningless that man must envy the animals and wish he had never been created. (A41 310ff, 373, A33 67, 81, 267, 126ff) The total solitude of hell almost inevitably overcomes the individual and drives him to some form of suicide, the final refusal or inability to love. The infinitude of Being is not an infinitude of love but an infinite void, a total absence of God which sucks in and consumes the individual. (A20 342, 358, A36 958, A30 227)

Most religions and philosphies see man in this tragic situation of imprisonment and isolation but prove to be unable to free the whole man from the guilt and death that cause the tragedy. Their usual solution is to sunder man into passing, passive matter and active, eternal spirit. (A33 72) The root of all evil, they say, is not freedom but either matter or spirit. Most say that the more the soul can extricate itself from the body and the illusory world of matter---from maya---, to that extent it will become immortal and free of all guilt, i.e. pure. (A31 176ff) The historical world and therefore man's unique person are the result of the soul's fall into the prison of the body. Thus both history and uniqueness must be left behind in order for the soul to return to its divine origin. (A30 314, A9 20f, A33 74ff) By withdrawing from matter, and therefore from history, the soul withdraws from all interpersonal relations and is immune to suffering. This refusal to suffer and denial of all personal distinction, however, makes love impossible. (A36 962) Above all sexual love is to be scorned for it leads only to an eternalization of death and guilt. (A31 196) Such Manichean systems are an attempt to preserve the glory of God and justify him by denying a dimension of reality that his glory is unable to penetrate and transform. (A36 222) They solve the problem of evil by declaring it a non-reality or a passing but necessary moment in the process of reunification with the divine.

The alternative solution is materialism which blames evil on the spirit, declares it a non-reality and strives to save man by freeing him from material want. They do it by reducing all reality to a univocal, formless, fully controlable matter. (A49 42, A34 45) Like Buddhism and Stoicism both solutions seek to pass beyond the reality of the individual bodily spirit who is subject to death and suffering. (B154 683) The modern philosophies of progress that deny either spirit or matter whether Hegelianism, Marxism or "Americanism" likewise can offer no ultimate justification for the dead individual left behind in the struggle for the future. Moreover they are often ruthless in their willingness to sacrifice the individual. (A47 129f, B154 685) They follow the age-old device of concentrating solely on the future in order to keep from facing the truest, deepest present evils of man. (A32 575)

50

If death remains the ultimate and evil is identified with the finitude of a material, individual body, salvation is inevitably sought in a return to complete identity with the divine spiritual origin. Any notion of a God distinct from the universe must be recognized as a passing illusion during this fallen state of individuality. (A33 76) It was shown above how frequent these philosophies and religions of identity are. Identity is sought, as in modern science, by way of abstraction from the concrete which in turn enables reason to free itself from and to gain control over univocal reality. (A34 44f) By proclaiming the act of abstraction to be the only proper relation to reality, they make ultimate reality knowable only as the needless absolute--never as personal love. (A40 23f) The more impersonal the divine is, the more readily man can seek identity with it. (A31 182) Man's freedom, therefore, is no longer understood as having been evoked by the Absolute Person and manifested in the response of his love to that person, but is itself designated as the Absolute and manifests itself in man's mastery of the universe. His insatiable desire to be both himself and all things, to be unique and universal, is both the evidence of his divinity and the cause of all his suffering. (A32 684f) He wages a Promethean struggle against any kind of distinct sovereign God and seeks to conquer the things of God without Him, before Him and in disobedience to His will; his life is dominated by the drive to murder God. (A32 745, A31 181)

Greek tragedy presents an attempt to find another solution to the problem of evil and death than that of a Promethean monism. It expresses clearly a strain in all Greek and Western thought that seeks to affirm the truth, goodness and beauty of all Being and to justify God in the face of human suffering without denying either matter or spirit. (A31 188, A36 122f, 96) Sophocles understands suffering and death as media of transcendence because the encounter with God as totally other tears him out of himself and gives his existence a new mid-point. (A36 117) Euripides rejects any notion of a God who abandons man in death and he points to certain victory over death through the lover's sacrifice of his life to preserve the life of the beloved. The great sadness that the sacrifice of Alcestis causes Admetus is overcome by a fairy-tale solution: Heracles brings Alcestis back to Admetus alive. (A33 68, A36 132ff) This is perhaps as close to the salvation of man and the justification of God through the death and resurrection of Christ that non-Christian religion and philosophy can come. Myths and fairy-tales mark out the place where revelation must take place but because they remain mere myths and fairy-tales, they show the impossility of man finding a solution to the problem of evil on his own. (A33 73) He is dependent on a divine solution that takes place in a specific form which man can understand as unique and divine. (A30 435) Without that form resignation in the face of death will never be the surrender of ones entire personal being into the hands of a personal Absolute Love. Not even the Israelites were able to do that. (A34 42f) Without that form an interpretation of the divine as Absolute Love will remain insane foolishness. (A34 46) As Thomas emphasized, if man has to rely solely on his reason---even a supernaturally finalized and illumined reason---he will remain for the most part in darkness. (S.c.G. I, 6.4)

Ebeling is fully in agreement with Balthasar that death is the crucial threat to a meaningful human existence. (G&W 60f) He sees death as the culmination of all things that rob man of his language and leave him with absolutely nothing to say. It rips open the context of all understanding and leaves man with no possibility of bridging the chasm by means of "language." In the face of death man no longer has the authority to say anything; no word that he speaks has the power to effect freedom. (24)

Gathering the Evidence

If death then does compel man to search for new evidence, he must begin laying new importance on his perception of form. He must cease to accept Kant's understanding of form as purely a construct of the mind and acquire a new reverence for the proper measure, inner-necessity and self-evidence of every form. In theology this means that new emphasis must be placed on "seeing" the form of Jesus. (A40 89ff) The theologians involved in the "New Quest for the Historical Jesus" are not taking up again the historicists' search for the "historical Jesus" but they do realize that if God reveals himself in Jesus in a way that is comprehensible and convincing for man, this revelation will occur in the full humanity of Jesus, in his full historicity. (25) It was the evangelists' desire to present the fascinating humanity of Christ that led them to incorporate their accounts of his life into the kerygma. They reacted against gnostic enthusiasts who were tending to ignore the concrete unique reality of Jesus and to turn Christianity into a system of ahistorical ideas and mythos. (26) They realized that an account of Jesus' life was necessary as a criterion and verification of the kerygma. (27) His words alone would lack the power of conviction if they were not seen to be "covered" by his existence. (A27 78, A30 192, 445) Christian faith would never find its ground in the fullness of his power unless it encountered his historical person. Merely hearing his teaching and that of his church is insufficient. (A30 472, 209, W&G II 70, 134, T&V 51) If Jesus is the logos, the word of God, his entire existence is that word, not merely his spoken words. (A28 32, 94, A32 635, W&G I 251) In this respect Jesus was no different than the Old Testament prophets who in Kierkegaard's words were also forced to "gesticulate with their entire existence." Like them, the fullness of his humanity makes him an image of God not just his words or the mere fact of his existence. (28) The entire Old Testament like the New Testament recounts God's deeds in history as performed by specific historical persons. (A46 253, A33 174)(29) God appears in their lives; the eschatological

(24) Ebeling, Theologische Sprachlehre, p. 126ff
(25) Kaesemann, Ernst, Exegetische Versuche und Besinnungen I, II Tuebingen, 1964, 1960 vol. I p. 194f, vol. II, p. 55
(26) Schweizer, Eduard, "Die Frage nach dem historischen Jesus," in Evangelische Theologie, 1964 p. 416
     Kaesemann, Ibid II p. 64ff;
(27) Kaesemann, Ibid II 68, Schweizer, Ibid 418, Ebeling, T&V 49
(28) Schweizer, Ibid p. 412
(29) Wright, G.E., God Who Acts, London, 1958 Third Edition

enters the depths of history and reveals itself there. (A28 166, A27 98ff, W&G II 133) In fact the fuller the revelation is the deeper it is hidden in the human. (A28 91) Therefore, the "that" of God, which for Bultmann is his eschatological call to decision, can be perceived only in the "what and how" of history. (T&V 69)(30) The contents and the act of revelation cannot be sundered from the form (A14 83, A30 144f, 158) or in Ebeling's words, the word cannot be sundered from its situation. (W&G II 182) The fullness of human communication must occur in the inseparable identity of word and deed. (W&G II 29f, G&W 40, A30 298f) Christ's revelation needs a corporal dimension and Christian theology must constantly resist the temptation to spiritualize it. (B18 98, A30 508, 416f)(31) Without the visible, objective body or form of Jesus, such spiritualism leads Christianity to subjectivism and the loss of community.(32) Moreover, Scripture and Christian faith itself lack all unity if such a form is not seen to unify the words and events of the New Testament and give them their meaning. (A30 155)(33) These events are not "eschatological" in the sense of ahistorical but are fully temporal and reveal the deeper meaning of time. (A32 840, A14 344ff)

Aesthetic contemplation of Christ's form, therefore, is the deepest act of faith and theology, as well as the noblest act of the human mind. (A28 250, A30 29, 166f, A47 56ff) It is the source of faith as a mode of understanding. It seeks understanding by bracketting blind faith, gathering together all the acts and teachings of Christ as contained in the witness of the apostolic church, comparing them with one another and seeking to find their inner unity, their all-encompassing form. (A32 225, 99, 50, A28 103, A30 493, A34 93f) The believer and the theologian strive to enter more and more deeply into the meaning of Christ's specific acts and teachings only in order to understand the person who is their common subject. In Origen's words the theologian seeks the "spiritual meaning" which he finds by "comparing spiritual things with other spiritual things." (cf 1 Cor. 2:13) It is this "speculative" theology that leads to the nucleus of the event and form that Christ is. (A46 92ff) It requires of the theologian more a seeing mind than a dialectical one. (A29 381) He must have the attentiveness of Goethe's eye, Hopkin's will to objectivity and pertinency (A32 727ff), Anselm's and Burckhardt's ability to trace carefully and rationally the contours of historical forms. (A30 448f, A32 225) With Irenaeus he must strive to see what is, to stand before the evidence of things, to describe their beautiful surface as the appearance of their depths, and to surrender himself to the evidence that appears. (A32 45f, 56) This means he would insist with Pascal on seeing the splendor of Christ's love. (A32 543) In order to do this Pascal maintained that

---

(30) Ebeling, "Das Natuerliche bei Luther" in Kirche, Mystik, Heilung und das Natuerliche bei Luther, Goettingen, 1967 p. 178
(31) Kaesemann, Ibid, vol I p. 202
(32) Ibid vol. II p. 68
(33) Ibid. vol. I p. 213

the use of concepts is less important for theological reasoning than participation in the spirit of geometry, than seeing order and form within the act of non-seeing faith. (A32 544) He does not merely compare images but orders all the apparently accidental historical aspects of Christ's existence around the incomprehensible splendor of the cross. This kind of logical reasoning leads to faith's rational certitude. (A32 228f, A30 578) The method of theological reasoning is, therefore, primarily one of induction that is totally dependent on a multitude of unique, concrete, apparently accidental words and deeds in history. (A30 157) The induction leads to a believing vision of God's word as a whole and a recognition of its identity with divine reason, so that the believer knows the word in all situations to be rational even when he cannot fully understand. (A30 133) Ebeling insists on this inductive, believing insight into the inner-necessity of the kerygma by stressing that the theologian must be able to show why the preaching Jesus had to become the preached Christ. (T&V 33) Both Kaesemann and Ebeling have stressed the necessity of this kind of vision over against Bultmann's rejection of any kind of contemplation. (33) Ebeling sees that Jesus has a definite form and that the theologian must strive for a vision of the risen Christ. (34)

It resembles the thought process the apostles underwent. Up until the resurrection they had seen in Jesus a "prophet great in word and deed," but they were forced by the resurrection to start rethinking all that Jesus had done and taught in order to discover why it was necessary that he be crucified and rise again. Through a phenomenological commitment to the reality that lay before them and in a process of induction that saw everything in Jesus' life and teaching converge upon the cross and resurrection with an ineluctable necessity, they came to see the cross as the definitive appearance of divine splendor. (A46 16, A40 65) They strove in the New Testament to delineate the form of Jesus the Christ in such a way that the reader will see why Jesus is the fullest possible appearance of God in history and why it is impossible to expect a greater prophet after him. The end and fulfillment of history cannot be a new revelation of God but only the return of Jesus the Christ.

The task of theology is to help others see-understand-verify the form that the apostles present. It must show why Jesus is absolutely unique, i.e. why he is the definitive appearance of God and the definitive relation between man and God. (A30 181, 447ff, A33 208f, A40 67) (35) This involves showing the inner-necessity of his form, i.e. why the constituents of his form must be present in exactly the way they are if his form is to be truly final. (A32 228) It must show how all the discrepancies and apparent contradictions in the New Testament are expressions of necessary

---

(34) Ebeling, Wesen des Glaubens, Tuebingen, 1959 p. 64, Eng. trans. The Nature of Faith, Fortress 1961; T&V 70.

(35) Kaesemann, Exegetische Versuche und Besinnungen I, p. 196.

tensions, proportions and balances within his total form. (A30 469) No one could affirm the New Testament witness without at least a sense for this uniqueness and inner-necessity. The theologian must, therefore, make this "sense" an increasingly explicit and defensible understanding. (A40 68f) His task is like that of the aesthetician who shows what the objective qualities of an art work are that merit for it the title of a masterpiece. (A30 171ff) He must point out the unique law or aesthetic logic which determines what elements constitute the art work and what proportions exist between the elements. (A30 158, 213, A28 127) The expert who can see this aesthetic logic sees the specific "values" of the colors and shapes whereas the layman sees only a familiar reality or a confusion of lines and colors. Its accidental uniqueness and originality are justified and grounded in its presentation of the greatest freedom as the most necessary. The more perfect, original and therefore free and self-measuring an art work, the more it compels the admirer to exclaim, "That's the only way it could be!" (A30 538, A28 194, A32 228, 217) Seeing the total form of a Bach fugue or a Mozart concerto one realizes that each movement and each theme has to be as it is, that to add or subtract a few tacts would violate the inner law that governed its development and constitutes its unity. The better the art work, the less its parts are merely fitting or proper and the more they speak of a binding inner-necessity. (A30 157)

Because the fittingness, correctness, symmetry, proper proportion, etc. in Christ's form is totally without fault and therefore the most perfect possible, it is impossible to distinguish this fittingness from an absolute necessity. (A40 67, A30 164, A32 25, 228) The basic proportions of Christ's form, the Trinity and the Incarnation, and the specific way in which they are revealed in his human love: his deeds, teaching, cross and resurrection, cannot be altered or eliminated by any process of de-mythologization without filling his form with contradictions and rendering it incredible. (A45 96, A30 468) A theologian can and must be able to show that any attempt to criticze this form shows only the inadequate vision of the critic, rather than the inadequacy of the form. (A30 165) He must be able to show the critic his blindness to the logic of love that governs the totally free relation between God's love and creation's response, (A46 102) and makes possible the fundamental theological "synthesis a priori": Jesus is the Christ, the Son of God. This logic of love makes it necessary for Christ to come and to have exactly the form that he has; it constitutes his inner-necessity and evokes man's insight into that necessity. The perfect proportion between the expressed and the expression, between his simplicity and profundity, gives his form such an exactitude, vividness, fullness, and weightiness that one is compelled to see its perfection. (A28 33) The perfect logic of his form makes it irresistible; its utter simplicity turns apparent contradictions in his image into fully appropriate tensions in the unity of the totality. (A30 470, A32 228) Each element of the form appears in the light of the totality, i.e. in the full splendor of Christ, as a postulate or logical conclusion that is fully natural, reasonable and necessary.

Christ's form acquires the greatest possible self-evidence in the splendor of this greatest possible necessity, perfection and freedom. Nothing could be more fascinating and more terrifying than Christ's form; nothing could more overwhelm the believer's aesthetic reason than Christ's beauty. (A32 237f) Faith understands and sees the form of Christ when it is overcome by the weight of divine love, by the sovereignty and authority of God's splendor, by "that than which nothing greater can be conceived." (A30 155f, 196f, A34 38, A39 62, C29 712) The inner-necessity of his form which is revealed in the faultlessness of its proportions, its correctness and appropriateness, shows the form to be the greatest conceivable. To be the greatest conceivable it must reveal the ground of its necessity in a totally free act of divine love. (A46 291f, A32 217) The gracefulness and freedom that appears in the inner-necessity of this form gives the form its splendor and thereby renders it self-evident. (A47 53, B69 457)

Christ's form possesses to the fullest degree the self-evidence and self-verification that characterize all love and beauty. (A30 409, A34 33ff, 83) His supreme manifestation of divine love and beauty allows a verification of his form that appeals ultimately neither to the fulfillment of some human need or expectation nor to merely historic, extrinsic events. (A30 446, 144) It verifies itself neither by submitting to any criteria or measures other than its own nor by requiring a blind leap of faith. (A30 110, 450) The objective splendor of the form can be understood by the subjective light of faith to be the highest conceivable form and yet it does not cease to be inconceivable. Biblical splendor has the power to make itself understood in its incomprehensibility; it can assert, prove and fulfil itself without losing its insuperable mystery. (A46 25) No human need or expectation can verify it because it is the epiphany of an unaccountable, ungroundable love which nothing in man can ground or account for.

Contents of the Form

Although it is the problem of death that creates in man the need to look beyond his a priori evidence to the new self-evidence of a unique form, he will not perceive this self-evidence if he remains focused on his need. The splendor of the risen Christ can be perceived only by one who is willing to follow Christ onto the cross, lose himself and forget his need. The self-evidence of beauty and love is apparent only to someone who is not asking what good the revelation will do him. It must be received as an overwhelming surprise that delights and terrifies him and in so doing makes even his concerns about death secondary. Although Christ does reveal God's love for us, the believer is enamored primarily by God's loveliness; although Christ does reveal God's ability and desire to free us, the believer rejoices primarily because God himself is freedom. As will be brought out in this section, the self-evident splendor of Christ lies primarily in the self-sufficient freedom and love between the persons of the Trinity and only secondarily in their love for creation. Intra-Trinitarian love and freedom are not merely the fulfillment of all human need but in Anselm's words are "such that nothing greater can be conceived" and "greater that what can be conceived." The Trinity infinitely surpasses the measure of human need and measures itself by its own measure.

Therefore, the Trinity is not beautiful and the form of Christ does not radiate its self-evidence primarily because Christ conquers death. Nevertheless without this conquest Absolute Love could not appear and could not be credible. Thus it will be necessary to show in addition to the evidence of the Trinity in itself, the evidence of

the Trinity's saving grace. His self-evidence is grounded secondarily in his ability
to establish a proportion between the most disproportionate of realities: the temporary and the everlasting, mortal man and immortal God. The symmetry uniting his
crucifixion and resurrection preserves them simultaneously within one form and
overcomes their contradiction. He rises with a body covered with wounds. The
wounds represent man at the moment he is most aware of his humanity, while the
risen body contains the eternal, all-powerful splendor of God. The fullness of finitude is united with the fullness of infinity yet not destroyed.

A. The Trinity in Itself

Christ's perfect oneness with God is revealed in human form by his perfect
obedience to his Father. In the eyes of the evangelists, Jesus' obedience to the Father gives unity to his entire life. Obedience causes him to remain behind in the
Temple and obedience characterizes his life in Nazareth. He "has to be" baptized
by John and receives there the Spirit who gives him his mission and drives him into
the desert to have his obedience to the Father tested. His temptation and his fidelity
to the Father's will characterize his public life and reach their climax in Gethsemani
and on Calvary. (A45 73) His whole life stands under the dei, the "it is necessary,"
of much suffering. (A45 15) His teaching revolves around the necessity of standing
poor, helpless, defenseless like a child before the Father and it is this unquestioning
faith of Abraham that will move the Father's heart and insure a hearing of his prayer.
(A46 123, 308f) This obedience proves his love for the Father and expresses the
immediacy of their relation. (A46 231, 309)

His total surrender to the Father is given its full expression in the passion,
the epitomy of his existence. (A46 63ff) This is the hour whose coming only the Father knows since the servant Jesus cannot survey his master's plan. (A46 133f, A43
8) His helplessness and ignorance of the future are expressed supremely in the naked confrontation of wills in Gethsemani. Here he most clearly consents to being
stripped by the Father of his own glory and his own form. In Gethsemani he prepares
to plunge himself into the total destruction of his own glory, word, and form. (A45
73f, A43 9, A46 138, 196) This ultimate humility and obedience is a turning over to
the Father of all the room in himself and a rejection of human glory in order to make
room for divine splendor. (A30 313, A46 349)

No human action could more fully express the union between Christ and his
Father than this total giving of his life at the Father's request. There is nothing
more that any human can give and thus no better way to unite the giver with the recipient. Yet this union is not simply one of identity. Christ's words in Gethsemani,
"not my will but yours be done," and his word on the cross, "Why have you forsaken
me?" clearly portray the lasting distinction between Christ and the Father.

If it were not for the resurrection, we would not see anything on the cross
but this separation. If it were not for the resurrection, death would be ultimate and
such total surrender to the Father would be suicidal. Because his wounded body is
raised up and glorified by the Father, first on the cross and later in encounters with
his followers, the most human in Christ, his mortality, becomes fully transparent

to the most divine, to his divine sonship. The splendor of God becomes visible, audible and touchable to the fullest extent possible in a human being. All the beauty of humanity is converted into obedient worship of the divine and thereby into the fullest possible revelation of the divine. (A36 473) All the human acts of Christ's life are united into a form and receive in the resurrection the final symmetry they had anticipated but seemed to have lost in the crucifixion. (A45 161f)

His mission, which is his form, is completed in the pouring out of blood and water from his wounded side and in the sending of the Spirit at Pentecost. He had come to reveal his union with the Father and that union is the Spirit. His mission is to reveal the interior life of the Trinity and he does this in his death and resurrection. He reveals the Father as the one who sent him on the mission and affirmed his mission; he reveals the Spirit as the one whom he sends to complete his mission. Christ reveals the Trinity in a form constituted by the Trinity itself. (A30 139, 147, A34 57, A46 15) The form of Christ reveals the Trinity to be itself something like what we know as form. A dim analogy does exist between form as we know it and the supra-form of the Trinity. (A32 288, A40 237, A30 415) The Father is the ground-less source, conceiver and expressor who exists in a tension with the Son who is his form, appearance, idea and expression. This tension is held together in harmony by the Spirit because the Son exists as giving himself back to the Father and glorify-ing him; the Spirit is the love that caused the Father to conceive the Son and the Son to surrender himself to the Father. (A40 95, A32 295ff, 671, A30 311, 588)

The form of the Trinity is beautiful because it is absolutely free, self-suffi-cient love. (A40 65, 95, A36 432) The splendor of the Trinity radiates from the boundless, graceful, playful mutual self-surrender between the Father and the Son. God is not under any of the binding necessities that most philosophies impose on him. He need not struggle and create in order to find himself rather He freely and gracious-ly gives and receives himself. Because he is within himself the identity of selfhood and otherness, he need not look outside of himself for an object of his love. (A32 502) Just as any love grows and becomes more beautiful the less it is grounded in need, so God's love is the most beautiful love conceivable because it is totally without need. Just as any love is more mysterious the freer it is, so God's love is boundlessly mysterious because of its boundless freedom. Therefore, it is precisely in the splen-dor of God, as boundless love emerging from the form of the Trinity, that the form of Christ has its objective evidence. It is Anselm's evidence of "that than which noth-ing greater can be thought," and "that which is greater than what can be thought." (A39 43f, A40 64f) The depths of Christ are inexhaustible, immeasurable, and un-surpassable because they are the splendor of a totally free love.

This splendor gives Christ an irresistability that compels men to leave ev-erything and follow him. This splendor gives him the fullness of power to forgive sins and to point to himself credibly as mankind's ultimate source of fulfillment or failure. His splendor is the authority that grounds all faith and therefore effects all salvation.

B. The Trinity as Savior

As Christ's union with the Father is revealed through his obedience, so his saving union with creation is revealed in his solidarity with man. He enters into the most human of situations, the isolation of death. He enters the situation that most profoundly challenges the child's interpretation of reality as Absolute Love. By doing so and having his wounded body raised and glorified, Christ makes the mortal transparent to the immortal. Thus all the finite forms that spoke to the child of immortal love regain the transparency they lost in the face of death. Christ's saving acts make the Trinitarian splendor visible in all forms. Salvation, therefore, is the condition for the possibility of verifying Christ yet not its ultimate ground. It is not our being loved by the Trinity that ultimately grounds his credibility rather the splendor of the Trinity's love for itself.

If Christ's obedience reveals his union with the Father, it is his willingness to take upon himself the isolation of death and all its consequences that reveals God's willingness to share man's fate. He is ready to accept God's responsibility for the consequences of the divine gift of freedom. (A32 254) Jesus spends his life sharing the isolation of society's exiles and scapegoats, the sick, the poor and the sinners. This sharing of human loneliness becomes total when Christ "loves to the end" on the cross. He shares man's radical estrangement from his roots and his destiny. Seeking to overcome this estrangement and to open to all men the possibility of sharing the intimate life of the Trinity, he must enter the situation of those who reject the life he offers. Because his offer of eternal life can be rejected, it opens to man the possibility of eternal death. Into the fullness of this eternal hell Jesus and Jesus alone must enter. He dies the second death that embraces all the loneliness of human deaths. He suffers the fullness of the divine anger as it is aroused by man's rejection of what he reveals. Like a sponge he soaks up pure sin in itself, sin as it has been abstracted from the whole of human history. (A45 36, 99ff, 123f)

With his final scream on the cross Jesus is reduced to wordlessness and formlessness; the cross is the end of all human beauty, of all human aesthetics. But through the glorification of his wounded body in the resurrection, the end of human aesthetics is made the mid-point of divine aesthetics. As was seen in discussing the need for a posteriori evidence, death is the epitomy of isolating evil and it most of all destroys the transparency of forms to the splendor of Absolute Love. The risen wounded body of Christ saves all mortal beauty by turning its very mortality into a revelation of Trinitarian love. (A36 38) His death becomes a manifestation of the weakness, foolishness and wastefulness of the divine heart. (A45 9, A46 126) It reveals a God who will love "to the end," who will go even further than Yahweh's pursuit of the whoring Jerusalem. (A47 130, A32 616, 867, A30 631) Death's silence is transformed into the supreme communication of Absolute Love. Death's isolation is transformed into the supreme communion of the mortal with the immortal, the sinner and the justified. (A32 578f) Death becomes the mid-point of a new supra-form and supra-word that reconciles the ultimate irreconcilables. (A46 135, 78, 196, 301) Jesus' death is an act of perfect obedience to the Father and total solidarity with man. As such it turns Christ himself into the perfect form of love between immortal God and his mortal creation. His very person becomes the form that unites God with all aspects of his creation. Jesus is the covenant.

Christ's potentiality as the covenant form uniting Creator and creature is
realized by the Spirit that Jesus breathes out on the cross with his final breath.
Christ is the form of the union, while the Spirit, as the act uniting Father and Son,
is the act uniting God and creation. (A27 48, A46 192, A45 77) The breaking of
Christ's form on the cross allows Jesus to send the Spirit who will create out of
creation a new form, who will raise out of Jesus' wounded body a new body in which
all can participate. As the Spirit of Christ and the Spirit of the Creator he has the
basically aesthetic task of making the form of Christ present to every individual in
every situation and thereby allowing each to be conformed to Christ in his own particular way. (A45 136, A30 318)

Because Christ has known the highest human act in his obedience and the
most desperate human situation in his abandonement by the Father, he has taken
man's measure and there is room in his form for every human experience. (A46
355, A45 12) He is entitled to save man by becoming man's new form, measure,
way, norm, law and rule. His form radiates a cauterizing love that by judging man
transforms him and enables him to participate in Christ's reconciliation of the Creator and the creature. By participating in the Son's mission from the Father
through the mediation of the Spirit, man draws creation to its source and end; he
shares in the interior life of the Trinity. (A36 398f, A30 462) As one conforms to
Christ's obedience to the Father and solidarity with man, he shares in the ultimate
truth and meaning of reality: the worship of the Father by the Son and the Spirit. The
Spirit's saving activity of conforming us to Christ means that he grounds us in the
Son who in turn grounds us in the Father. Conformation to Christ's humanity is
impossible without conformation to the Trinity. (A21 49f) Because his basic form is
that of the Incarnation, one can be conformed to Christ only by sharing the form of
the Trinity. (A46 292)

a. The Trinity Fulfils Creation

By enabling creation to be proportioned to the Trinity, Christ offers to creation a fulfillment that is both the highest conceivable and higher than conceivable.
This constitutes a major portion of his objective evidence.

He is able to fulfil creation from within because the revelation of Absolute
Love in his created humanity is analogous to the revelation of Absolute Being in all
created forms. (B18 102f, A28 191ff, 125) Both appear as the hidden, magnificent
ground in expressive forms. Christ's solidarity with all creation means that his
new word obeys the laws that govern all words; his word is written into the word
of contingent Being and the words of all finite beings. (A36 959ff, A28 174ff, A30
291f, 415) Therefore, he is able to save creation from inside. By virtue of the analogy of Being all created forms can share in his worship of the Father and in his
revelation of Absolute Being as the Absolute Love of the Trinity. (A32 9, A30 33f)

Through Christ's emptying of himself into the human situation the light of the
Trinity is poured out into the depths of all beings and begins to shine there. The
splendor of the Trinity does not consume the finite being with brilliance but gives it
the freedom to express itself fully. (A32 295, 347f) Unique created forms are not

simply reabsorbed into the uncreated One and annihilated but participate in Christ's created humanity. The proportion between Creator and creation that is established in the Incarnation prevents forms from being destroyed in their union with the divine. Grace does not destroy nature; redemption does not destroy creation, but through the created humanity of Christ each unique created form is called to share with the Son his role as image, appearance and glorification of the Father. (A36 313ff, A32 750f, 640, 116f, 81) The distances between the persons of the Trinity and between the humanity and divinity of Christ make room for a fulfillment of the creature without out a total loss of distance between itself and the Creator. The relation will remain one of a dialogue of love and not be reduced to an identity. (A31 37f) Because of these two proportions, the Trinity and the Incarnation, the universe is called with the Son to reflect the Father by flowing out from him and surrendering itself back to him. Christ's perfect union of two natures allows him to become the supreme example for all beings and thus turns his exemplarism into the key to all metaphysics. His mission from the Father and return to him becomes the ultimate interpretation of the egress and regress that dominates all metaphysics. (A31 355ff, A14 269ff, A36 339) The dynamic forms of the Incarnation and Trinity replace and fulfil the return of multiple being to the measureless, formless One of neo-Platonic, Hindu, and Idealist metaphysics. (A31 187f) The ultimate reconciliation of all things that every metaphysics envisages becomes in Christ a harmony and symphony filled with tensions and proportions held in balance by the power of love. (A32 73, 577f) The splendor of love and not the melting of all forms into a oneness without shape and proportion and splendor, becomes the ultimate interpretation of Being. (A34 92ff) For this reason Christianity is the absolutely aesthetic religion. (A30 208)

b. The Trinity Fulfils Humanity

Because the ultimate truth of Being is a form constituted by the free personal relations of the Trinity and because this form is revealed in the free personal form of Christ's humanity, it offers to each person the highest conceivable fulfillment of his unique freedom. This overwhelming regard for the preciousness of personal freedom constitutes another crucial part of Christ's splendor and objective evidence.

Christ's similarity to all human forms is a precondition for our understanding his revelation of Absolute Freedom and Personality. All human forms transform the analogy of Being into an analogy of freedom and personality, thereby making human forms transparent to the freedom and personality of Absolute Being. By becoming man the Son chooses this mode of revelation to portray the freedom and personality of the Trinity. (A28 63, A27 13ff) Therefore, the man who is able to perceive something like absolute personal freedom in the poor and suffering as well as in geniuses, heroes, kings and saints has the preparation necessary to perceive Christ's Trinitarian revelation. (A32 765, A40 294) Ebeling sees the similarity of Christ's evidence to the claim of the poor and suffering on our help, but he is reluctant to see any similarity between Christ's fullness of power and the power and splendor of great men. Nevertheless he does vigorously insist that an essential part of Christ's credibility lies in the human quality of his revelation. (W&G II 32, 41, G&W 33, 91) Balthasar on the other hand is much less reluctant to stress the similarity between

Christ's splendor and that of the heroes, prophets, poets and saints of history. Christ's word recapitulates the language of all natural forms as well as all human forms. He speaks the language of the body as well as the spirit; he speaks the language of Mesopotamia and Egypt as well as Israel; he speaks the language of infancy, childhood and adolescence as well as of manhood. (A32 802, A28 69, 94, 76ff) The word of God is poured out into every aspect of his humanity so that it can transform all aspects of humanity into manifestations of his splendor.

This analogy between Christ's revelation and the revelation in all human forms is further intensified in the similarity of his revelation to that of the great religious figures. (A28 59ff) Their fidelity to the Absolute is similar to Christ's obedience to the Father and their roles as representatives of the people are similar to his solidarity with mankind. (A32 799f, 754) Not only the great figures of Israel but also their Babylonian and Egyptian counterparts as well as Odysseus, Oedipus, Socrates and Aeneas help to prepare mankind for the vision of Christ's form. (A40 348ff) No matter how unique Jesus may be, he and his religion will always remain rooted in and presuppose the natural religious structure of mankind. (A36 93ff, A30 477ff, A40 356)

The splendor of his love surpasses the splendor of all the theophanies that anticipate him. He fulfils all myth and religion by personalizing and historicizing it. (A36 898ff, A29 369, A46 146, A30 226, 478, A28 125) As the climax of God's revelation of his personal love in the concreteness of history, he is the ultimate union of mythic transcendence with the this-worldliness of history. (A30 484) The attempt of myth to reveal the transcendent in personal images is absolutized in Christianity's bond to a very concrete, specific individual in history. (A32 758) Christianity not only starts with the sensible but demands continued hearing, feeling and tasting of the Absolute in the sensible, in flesh and blood. (A30 302) Greek tragedy epitomizes this concreteness of myth and most clearly prefigures Christ by remaining steadfastly and defenselessly open to the incomprehensible will of the transcendent and yet in the depths of the concrete historical situation.. (A36 94f) By becoming more intimately present in history, the transcendent in Christ becomes endlessly more historical and incomprehensible than in Greek tragedy. The relation in Christ between a specific historical man and a personal God becomes the revelation of an I/Thou relation within God himself. In the concreteness of Christian revelation myth is fulfilled; in the historicity of Christianity myth is surpassed. (A30 139) Christ can reveal these personal depths of the Trinity concretely because he takes history even more seriously than Greek tragedy. He has an even greater sensitivity to true human love, to the tragic defeat of love by hate, treason and death as well as to the hidden splendor of love beyond all visible success. (A34 95f) It is precisely this sensitivity to the depths of human history that enables Christ to gather in his form all pagan deities and all the logoi spermatikoi scattered in the multitude of myths. (A30 483, A36 33) His humiliation and his glorification resume all the oriental myths about a primal man, his fall and his return to unity. (A30 609) Christ's father fulfils all the images of gods who become caught up in the tragedy of man. (A33 87) He concretizes the abstract ways of mysticism and his word assumes and fulfils its holy wordless silence. (A33 257, A29 378) All Asian submission to an impersonal natural law is fulfilled by personal obedience to Absolute Love. (A28 368)

This fulfillment of myth and philosophy is concretized in Christ's fulfillment of Israel. Israel had already fused the mythic forms of the Orient with the philosophy of Greece into a unique religion. Her theology revolves around various great religious forms she has synthesized but because they lack a unifying mid-point she finds no final meaning in herself and remains a puzzle. (A41 224, A40 22, A30 629) Her final meaning can be found only in her preparation of the forms that Christ will synthesize in his form. (A32 81, A30 602ff, 610f) She prepared for the form of the king who is historical and represents all of his subjects; and that of the Suffering Servant, who dies for his people; and that of the Son of Man, who is divine. (A30 608f) Seeing the synthesis of these forms in Christ demands an aesthetic sensitivity to spiritual proportions. (A30 634) With it one can see that Christ is the true reality of the shadowy, promisory images of Israel, and that through Israel God had begun imposing the form of Christ on history. (A41 371ff) Here lies the source of the dynamism in Christ's form. Because the whole of history is present in the dynamic relationship between the long history of Israel and Yahweh, and because Christ absorbs Israel, he absorbs the whole history of the relation between the passing and the eternal. (A40 302, A30 315)

Having been absorbed and fulfilled by Christ, all the forms of history can serve to train the eye of the believer to behold the fully human evidence of Christ's splendor. They teach him how to make the fully human response necessary for understanding Christ's form. Because his human splendor is a profound intensification of the gratuitous and thus in some way personal beauty revealed by all forms, his intense freedom and personhood radically intensify the experience of freedom and personhood given by all forms. Without having received this intensified freedom man cannot even perceive Christ's form. (B46 118, A32 503, A33 260) The turning of the Trinitarian persons to man gives rise to the new person necessary to appreciate Christ's splendor. (B5 847, A46 375, A32 501f) Thus Christ's fully human splendor draws the full range of man's humanity onto a new level. No part of man's humanity is forced to respond and thus no part is left behind. God has sunk his word so profoundly into the human that it remains hidden in the human and thus can elicit a free response rather than demand it. Once the believer has put together all the elements of Christ's form and correlated it to his own situation, he may be overwhelmed by the splendor that emerges. He may find it impossible to resist the claim that Christ makes and be compelled to obey. But even then his freedom is not violated. Even though the receptive side is primary and freedom consists primarily in responsibility, obedience, endurance and dependence, the individuality of the believer is not destroyed. Precisely because the form of Christ radiates a free, playful, gracious splendor, the Spirit can bring Christ's form into each unique situation in a unique way and achieve a unique conformation. At every moment and in each situation the believer is confronted with an image of himself that draws him closer to his unique mode of conformation to Christ.

For this reason neither the most insignificant moment nor the most fleeting situation needs to be excluded from the final synthesis in Christ's form. Nothing on the horizontal plain is incapable of being gathered up and united on the vertical plain. (A32 548) The most public, profane, political and economic moments can be harmonized with the most personal, intimate and sacred ones in Christ's form. (A33 55,

211, A21 54f, A46 354) There is no moment, no place and no particular person that has to be left behind. All can play the role of Beatrice and lead Dante right into the very Kingdom of God. (A32 388)

Thus eternity is to be found in the moment and above all in those moments when we swear eternal love to another. Such an oath no longer needs to be dispelled as a romantic illusion. All our personal relationships receive eternal significance through their inclusion in the form that personally unites Christ with mankind and with the Father. No one is prevented from becoming a form radiating the splendor of the Trinity. (A28 91f, A32 756) Every human form can participate eternally in the divine self-communication that is the meaning of history and the meaning of eternity. (A30 655, A36 485) The divine artist can gather all the scattered fragments of Adam and restore through the fire of his love the original unity of mankind in a single human nature. (A6 57, 112, A33 49) No one needs to be excluded and damned eternally to hell except Christ himself; he alone is predestined to hell. Christ has not removed the threat of hell for any individual rather he first opens this possibility by enabling man for the first time to know the unconditional yes he receives from God. Only this knowledge makes it possible for man to say an eternal no. (A34 60) But by himself undergoing this eternal hell Christ reveals a Father's heart that cries over his prodigal son and goes in search of a lost lamb. By himself suffering eternal damnation God opens the possibility of freeing himself from the anxiety of having to exclude a single person. (A32 861, 867, A47 86, A46 382, 414, A14 188)

Christ's ability to thus reveal a Father who respects human freedom but is able and willing to rescue every moment, every situation and every form from eternal death, makes his splendor irresistible. Not only does he demonstrate that the ultimate reality of the universe is fully spontaneous, unconditioned love, but he makes that love, which is believable in itself, also believable for us by showing it to be all-inclusive. Because his form has room in it for all other forms, its splendor gives it irresistible objective evidence. It has the evidence of being both the "greatest conceivable" and "greater than conceivable."

Chapter Three

THE EXPERIENCE OF THE THEOLOGIAN

Contemplation, Action, Worship

In addition to the objective evidence of Christ's splendor the theologian must also depend on his own subjective evidence. What happens to him when he is overwhelmed by Christ's irresistible splendor plays an essential role in the credibility of his theology. In considering the subjectivity of the theologian it will be imperative first to disarm the profound Protestant mistrust of theological aesthetics. Luther, Kant, Kierkegaard and Bultmann, to name a few, have made it their most basic methodological task to overcome the division of theory and practice. The great spectre in their eyes is speculation, theory, seeing, contemplation, mysticism or any form of knowledge that threatens to prescind from decision. Therefore, it is precisely the aesthetic moment of free, playful, "useless" interchange between seer and seen that is so suspect for them. They fail to realize that the moment of contemplative distance between seer and form, although crucial, is not the whole of aesthetics. Beauty cannot be fully experienced without hearing a call to decision and a change in one's life.

Contemplation

Balthasar's theological aesthetics is one with the Protestant tradition in insisting on the experiential character of all theological understanding. The theologian is totally dependent on an experiential knowledge of God in which his whole person vibrates and resonates. (A30 235, A40 41, A30 238) To be wise he must taste, as the Latin word for wisdom indicates. (A32 510, 275, A21 86f) No books can teach him the science of experience necessary to teach and no understanding of a text is possible without experiencing there the actuality of revelation. (A30 276, A32 490)

The objectivity of theology is obtained by experiencing Christ in such a way that one is led to share his perspective. The more thoroughly a theologian is conformed to Christ's unconditional obedience to the Father and unconditional solidarity with mankind, the more objective his theory will be. (A30 594, A34 54, A28 217, A19 448) It is in practice that theory becomes objective. Balthasar and Ebeling are in agreement that the very distinction between theory and practice---although it stretches back to Patristic theology and is the most acute problem facing theology today--- is a sign of decadence. (A28 209, A47 26, A10 289) This decadence becomes especially obvious in scholastic theology with its sundering of dogmatic from spiritual or mystical theology. The daily life of the laity, the concrete tasks of the clergy and the experiences of the mystics and saints cease to be sources for dogmatic theology. As a result dogmatic theology comes to have little relevance for the life of the church. Balthasar is grateful to Luther for recognizing not only that the distinction between theoretical and practical theology is impermissable but that the very distinction between a theologian's theoretical and practical responsibilities is unacceptable. (A47 35, A31 41ff, A30 577f, 71ff) There must be a constant, fructifying interchange between the two. Because Christ is himself both theory and practice, theory and spirituality cannot be distinguished. (A43 16, A47 21, 27f, A40 242) Ebeling likewise stresses that an important aspect of his theory of language is its transcendence of the distinction between theory and practice.(35) The pure theory, speculation, objective seeing that the Protestants reject, Balthasar is also willing to label demonic. (A31 332)

Nevertheless, to say that there is no pure theory is not to say with Bultmann that there is no room for contemplation, reflection and imagination. The great importance of practice for understanding must not lead to an identification of decision and understanding. Balthasar would agree with Kaesemann that such an identification would mean proposing rape as the model of understanding.(36) It is true that there can be no understanding without love, and contemplation unlike pure theory is an act of love. It is a loving gathering of evidence and an observation of that evidence until it crystalizes into a form. Unless the theologian has learned to do this with all forms, he will be blind to the Trinitarian splendor of Christ. Christian theology must acknowledge its dependence on something like Plato's use of mythic forms or Goethe's morphology if it is to explicate the uniqueness of Christ's form to the world. (A30 430, A36 16) It is dependent on a philosophy that convinces the human heart it will grow and progress not primarily by technology but by the loving, reverent contemplation of forms. (A36 980ff) Technology can contribute to human progress only by freeing man for the act of contemplation. If man's vision were to be limited to the neutral, objectifying technological vision, it would be impossible for man to "see" the objective form of Christ. Therefore, a continuity such as Irenaeus and Hopkins found, must be maintained between the philosophical and the Christian vision of forms. (A32 764, 81)

All contemplation requires reason's concepts and categories for its full understanding and explication. Christianity has been notorious for its reliance on philosophy to present its contemplation to non-first-century, non-semitic peoples. (A28 95, A36 287) The New Testament authors make use of Hellenistic popular philosophy and the early councils use Greek philosophy. (A46 96, A36 281, 222) Even Barth is fully aware of this radical dependence and borrows himself liberally from various philosophical traditions. (A14 107)(37) An irrational faith is not a fully human faith and, as the history of Protestantism clearly shows, it inevitably leads to a monism in which reason transcends faith to an absolute knowledge. Reason both within and without Christianity must be seen not as the antithesis of faith but as grounded in and illumined by faith. (W&G II 279, A32 631). Reason exercises a philosophical faith on its way to

(35) Ebeling, Theologische Sprachlehre, p. 195
(36) Kaesemann, "Zum Thema der urchristlichen Apokalyptik" in Zeitschrift fuer Theologie und Kirche, 59 1962 p. 258.
(37) Barth, Karl, Kirchliche Dogmatik, IV 3, Zuerich, 1967, p. 842

Being and is ultimately in search of Absolute Being. (A29 367) The logic of God's revelation in Christ, therefore, is analogous to all human logic. (B48 213) Theology's rationality is the will to see this analogy. (38)

Equally as crucial as the role of reason in the contemplation of forms is the role of the human imagination. All theophanies are carved into the imagination and Christ's is no exception. (A30 482) The Christian depends radically on his ability to imagine Christ and to find images that express the Christian experience of divine splendor. The church fathers and Dante among others made abundant use of the classical images for this purpose. (A32 426ff, A36 286) These images served as a monstrance to illumine the phenomenon of Christ in the images of scripture. (A28 211, A36 288, A30 524)

The theologian who does not have the patience to practice such contemplation, reflection and imagination in his study of scripture, tradition and the contemporary situation will never perceive Christ's form and its particular evidence. He will constantly project his needs into his image of Christ and thus reduce Christ's credibility to his ability to fulfil those needs. Without receptive contemplation the theologian will be reduced to carrying on a monologue and is in grave danger of a solipsistic monism.

Action

Because contemplation is an act of love, it will inevitably lead to a decision and to action. The very act of seeing involves a decision to respond to one's experience of being seen. The believer sees Christ's form only when he knows himself seen, loved and measured by Christ and decides to respond. (T&V 46, A14 232ff) Seeing is a personal response to a personal act of love revealed in Christ's form and it involves love, obedience, conversion, enrapture, sanctification and conformation. (A30 316f, 502ff, 273ff, A46 201, 267) Christ's love includes the divine decision to save and the splendor of such love has an urgency that will not tolerate the neutrality of a curious spectator. (A46 26, 107, 168, 316, 155f) Man's decision is so urgent because objectively he has already been included in the divine decision.

The Christian, therefore, knows himself subjected to a divine imperative which he is able to understand only if he possesses the capacity for metaphysical wonder. This wonder that grounds philosophical aesthetics contains an imperative to respond to the splendor of Absolute Being. Presupposing this philosophical response to the divine imperative, the theologian can move on to a full understanding of the imperative emanating from Christ's form. This understanding must then itself be an act of life, of self-surrender, of faith, hope and love for Christ. (A28 159)

---

(38) Fuchs, Ernst, Marburger Hermeneutik, p. 182

The theologian must not only draw on the writings of the saints, he must himself be a "saint." (A28 282, A32 170) Both Congar and Schillebeeckx are dangerously misleading in their minimizing the relevance of the theologian's personal piety for his theology.(39) They ignore the insistence in the Johannine writings and in the works of Ignatius of Loyola on the identity of knowledge and life: truth is had only by him who walks in it, keeps Christ's word and loves his brother. (John 8:32, 2 John 1-4; A28 195, 203, A30 594, A47 58, A12 41) Surrendering oneself totally to the service of Christ is the only way to see the fullness of his power. (A30 105, T&V 97f) Dante's realization of his own truth by living his life out of love for Beatrice and his constant drawing on these personal experiences for his theology should be a model for all theologians. (A32 407) Likewise John of the Cross has a totally different kind of knowledge because he has been initiated into the mystery through love. (A32 474) Bonaventure in turn insists that the movement from science to wisdom can and must be achieved by following Christ. (A32 283) For the church fathers and medieval monks, philosphy-theology was identified with the consequent living of the Christian life either in the world or the monastery. It implied asceticism, total commitment and the readiness to be martyred---all for the sake of a "theoretical" goal, i.e. the knowledge of Christ. (A29 349ff) Without such an actively lived total surrender and an a priori acceptance of whatever is revealed, the theologian cannot see the infinite manifesting itself in the finite letter and flesh. (A28 159f) The sources of theology will remain closed books to him. Action alone renders his thoughts real and interior to him. (A6 141ff) Justice will remain unknown to him unless he acts justly. Since he cannot know God's work without doing it, his vision of revelation is the fruit of his works. (D2 342f) The basic disposition of his thought must be his desire to witness with his entire subjectivity. (A14 100f) Having heard the word of God and seen his splendor he cannot help but act.

Because understanding is impossible without action, it is obvious that the theologian cannot hope to convey the splendor of the Trinity convincingly to others unless his life is conformed to Christ's. His life must radiate the splendor of the Trinity in that his thoughts and desires are realized in deeds. (A47 27, 37) Bultmann goes so far at one point as to suggest that possibly understanding of existence can be communicated by the silent deed, that perhaps we must ultimately refrain from using words. Ebeling is basically in agreement except that he would draw deeds into his understanding of the "word-event." (W&G II 371) The theologian's words are often valueless unless he is able to speak to another from within by entering that person and assuming their guilt. (A47 61f) Henri de Lubac would seem to recognize in Balthasar such a unity of thought and deed and thus a transparency in his theology. He says about Balthasar's style that the reader of his works is led to a personal

---

(39) Congar, Yves, "Theologie," in Le Dictionnaire de la Theologie Catholique, XV, p. 470
Schilebeeckx, Edward, Offenbarung und Theologie, Mainz 1965, p. 88

encounter with God. (40) Such an encounter is the goal of all theology but if the theologian himself has not allowed the Spirit to form in him the proportions of Christ's form, he will be marred by such misproportions as childish optimism or morose pessimism and thus lose his credibility. (A28 269) Ebeling is, surprisingly for a Lutheran, once again in agreement with Balthasar, that theology is incredible without the theologian's correspondence to Christ's basic disposition and without his existence becoming an image of Christ. (T&V 88f, W&G I 212, A30 213) Both agree that neither the theologian himself nor anyone else can verify his theology without the criterion of his holiness, the fruits of his faith, his experience of revelation's saving, freeing, certifying power. (W&G II 32, 50, G&W 54, 60f) Just as the great interpreter must share the genius of the artist, so too the theologian must share the genius of Christ. Like the interpreter he can convey the uniqueness of the masterpiece only through the uniqueness of his personality.

<u>Worship</u>

The theologian's contemplation and decisive action receive their final form in the act of worship. Worship is the all-inclusive, unifying act that ultimately allows him to find true understanding. Just as only the lover and the beloved can understand their love, so too only the theologian who surrenders himself worshipfully to the Trinity can begin to understand the love that unites the persons of the Trinity and unites the Trinity with its creation. (A30 354, 594, A46 102, 379f, A28 217)

The roots of this worship lie in the act of wonder before the splendor of Being. The desire to celebrate the Trinity can arise only in someone who celebrates the splendor of Absolute Being. Therefore, any tendency to factualize and conceptualize reality must have been overcome by an awareness of the contingency and questionableness of Being. Because Christ's revelation is an answer to the ontological question provoked by this awareness, anyone who has not felt compelled to ask why there is Being rather than nothingness cannot understand, see or celebrate the splendor of Christ. (B48 210ff, A40 283ff, W&G II 249)(41)

Far from being dispensed from the pain and ecstasy of metaphysical wonder, the Christian must perform the act himself and even pressure philosophy to continue seeking to evoke it in others. (A36 980ff) For it is this wonder before the contingency of Being that evokes an awareness of the gratuity, graciousness and splendor of Being and thus enables the initial contact with Christ's splendor. (A36 964ff) The same Ebeling who insists that the encounter with the mystery of reality is ultimately an

---

(40) de Lubac, Henri, "Temoins du Christ," in <u>Civitas</u>, 1965 p. 588 (the entire issue is in honor of Balthasar)
(41) Fuchs, Ibid. p. 61

encounter with law that evokes fear and despair is nevertheless able to speak of reality being seen as a gift of the creator evoking joy, satisfaction, trust, thankfulness and wonder. (W&G II 38, 246, 302, G&W 47f) Metaphysical wonder is for him too a kind of faith that is not without analogy to Christian faith. (W&G II 200ff) (42) Christian faith must have its roots in this sensitivity to the night, the earthly, the intimate and hidden, the unexpected and the incomprehensible. (W&G II 206 390f)

Christ offers to this philosophical sense of wonder victory over the threat of an all-knowing, all-conquering reason. By removing in his death and resurrection all the objections against love as the ultimate meaning of reality, Christ removes all darkness from the splendor of Being and thus overcomes the rebellion, resignation and cynicism that threaten to suffocate wonder and eros. (A36 26f) The philosophical eros finds its fulfillment in the love between Christ and his bride. (A29 383) Christ is the greatest possible answer to the ultimate philosophical question about the why of Being. (A30 151, A40 289) Thus all celebrations of the Absolute can see themselves transformed and preserved in Christ. (A30 480ff) All erotic ascent to the Absolute is caught up and preserved by Christ's agape, which is the eros of the Absolute descending to man. (A32 654) He gives all the inchoative ways and forms of love, which threatened to become lost in the labyrinth, their true transcendent ground: Absolute Love in itself, i.e. the Trinity. (A34 94)

Rooted in such wonder the theologian is prepared to acknowledge that his celebration of the Trinitarian mystery will be necessary for him to understand its meaning. Evagrius goes so far as to declare an identity of prayer and theology: "If you are a knower of God (theologus) then you truly pray; and if you truly pray, you are a theologian." (B11 37ff, A29 381) The church fathers insist that the theologian "pray always" so that his style is able to evoke in the reader a response of worship. (A28 224) The extent to which a theology is prayed and prayable becomes an important criterion for its verification, since what theology truly means is what it means to the person who draws it into his prayer. (W&G I 350f) (43) The whole meaning for instance of the relation between the freedom of the will and the necessity of grace can be understood only in prayer. (B69 457)(44)

The heart of this worship is the theologian's attempt through his self-surrender to offer the Spirit a virginal womb that sets no preconditions and obstacles in the way of his inspiration. The theologian must "hang with all the fibers of his heart on every word that comes from the Lord's lips." The more deeply he participates in

(42) Ebeling, Vom Gebet, Tuebingen, 1963, p. 40
(43) Schaefer, Rolf, "Gott und Gebet" in Zeitschrift fuer Theologie und Kirche 65 1968, p. 122
     Ebeling, Vom Gebet, p. 122
(44) Pesch, Otto, "Existentielle und Sapientiale Theologie," in Die Theologische Literaturzeitung 92, 1967, p. 739.

Christ's worship, the freer the Spirit is to do what he wills with the theologian and the more nourishment the Spirit can give to his theology. (A28 164, A16 25) Ebeling expresses the same thought when he says worship is the only appropriate atmosphere or situation for theology. (G&W 63, W&G II 12)

Nevertheless, prayer is never to be reduced to a means for a deeper understanding, since adoration is a goal in itself and the highest goal of theology. (A21 95, A32 111f, A40 304ff) Nor can theological thought be reduced to the dialogue of prayer, since God is also beyond dialogue. He is not a finite partner but the not-other who is more interior to the theologian than his own interiority. (A32 111f)

The dependence of theology on prayer also does not mean that the theologian is unable to grow in understanding. Because of his prayer the Spirit is able to lead the theologian to a deeper and deeper understanding of revelation. This results in a certain esotericism and relativism in theology. Just as the beginner cannot see the excellence of a great masterpiece, so too the theologian who has not been sufficiently conformed to Christ by the Spirit and purified, cannot understand the truth perceived by a theologian more attuned to the Spirit. (A25 71, D2 33f) The theologian is forced to understand revelation according to the stage of development he has reached. What is true for one might be false if taught by another. It is for this reason that the medieval theologians insisted that the prospective theologian not begin his study until he had proved the solidity of his faith by his way of life and his wisdom. (A32 222, A30 275) Origen insists that only those who have conformed their lives to Christ's are worthy to theologize; only those who have fulfilled the commandment of love are worthy to receive from the Spirit the gifts of wisdom and science. (D2 137f, 157ff) The rejection of this esotericism after the Middle Ages led to the sundering of dogmatic and spiritual theology and to the profound impoverishment of both. Worst of all, the dogmatic theologian has tended more and more to lose the awareness of theology as a dynamic process in which he is constantly underway from the crucifixion to the resurrection. Like Luther he tends to isolate one particular moment of the process and to build his system on that. One powerful experience becomes the interpretive key to the whole of revelation instead of the theologian keeping in mind the whole range of experiences and the various levels of development that make a closed system impossible. (A14 87f, A45 194, A40 329, A34 54, A6 142f) As long as theology is a process and the Spirit is its primary driving force, the totally unforeseeable that bursts every system must be reckoned with. Every time a theologian thinks he has finally understood, he must be ready for a radical reminder that he knows nothing. He must be ready for the Spirit to expropriate all of his previous understanding and his entire life.

Expropriation

Expropriation, the allowing of one's smaller self to be possessed by the larger self of Christ, lies at the heart of the theologian's contemplative, active, worshipful response to the splendor of Christ's form. All beauty causes man to "stand outside of himself" (ec-stasy) and the splendor of the Absolute causes him to "stand in God" (en-thusi-asm). Being torn out of himself causes the Christian to lose his former subjective evidence while coming to dwell in God fills him with a new subjective evidence. These two experiences play a crucial part in the theologian's verification of his theology.

This ecstasy and enthusiasm have been constantly misinterpreted to mean the destruction of man followed by his re-creation out of nothing as a divine being. The discussion of the impact of grace on nature, and the impact of faith on reason has continually issued in a monism of grace and faith. As we have seen above (p. 5 ff, 12ff), such a monism means the ultimate destruction of all finite forms and thus the end of aesthetics and the loss of transcendence.

As part of his attempt to prevent this from happening Balthasar dwells on the significance of a strictly formal notion of pure nature. Although no human being has ever existed outside of the supernatural horizon opened by Christ's call, one cannot equate human existence with either implicit or explicit Christian faith. The revelation that creates faith is not a creation out of nothingness. There is a purely natural self which, although it has never existed as such in isolation, must be posited by theology as the recipient of Christian revelation. This nature stands in a paradoxical relation to grace. Although it must be capable of some true fulfillment without grace, in order for grace to be a free gift, yet, on the other hand, nature must absolutely require grace or grace would be superfluous. (A14 313, 354f) If grace were either totally extrinsic and superfluous to human nature or else absolutely necessary, man would in both cases cease to participate as a human in the Trinity and would instead become God. Salvation would mean God's necessary fulfillment of himself.

If grace were superfluous, man would be essentially constituted by his participation in the life of the Trinity; knowing the Trinity would ultimately be knowing himself. If grace, on the other hand, were in no way gratuitous, humanity would be reduced to pure need, sinfullness, nothingness and sin. Sin as the essence of humanity would be the sole distinction between God and man. Grace would be necessary to bring man into existence and thus his very existence would be grace or faith. In other words, if there were no human nature to be transformed by grace, all knowledge of the Trinity would have to be an unmediated, non-contemplative sharing in God's self-knowledge. (A14 294ff) A radical transformation of the human would no longer be necessary. Grace would become the nature of man, substantial instead of modal. The deepening of faith would no longer imply either a deepening of one's humanity or of one's awareness of the transcendent. (A14 302, 297f) Thus it would become the task of the theologian to shed himself of everything human in order himself to become a moment of divine self-knowledge. (A36 404f) Protestant theology has been dominated by a back and forth between these two paths to monism, because it has refused to discuss the capacity of pure human nature, i.e. formal nature uninfluenced by sin and grace. It has refused to acknowledge the goodness of its own createdness and thus implicitly refused to know its God as its Creator. (A14 173, A40 33)

Only if the capacity of pure nature to know God is acknowledged, can the theologian see that neither is he divine nor must he destroy his humanity but that grace draws him ecstatically out beyond his natural potential; it vastly overburdens him and thus plunges him into a dark night of the soul. The fact that his human nature is

fallen and must be transformed does make the process of knowing God excruciating.
But this sinfulness, need and nothingness do not make a distinctly human knowledge
of God impossible. The theologian need not abandon his humanity. He remains the
distinctly human agent of his distinctly human participation in the Trinity. The constant dying and rising of his humanity with Christ make his humanity suitable for
participation. Therefore, he must allow his humanity to be expropriated; he must
be ready to drop all of his present desires and insights as criteria in order to follow
Christ into an inscrutable darkness. The fulfillment of his present needs and insights
can never become the ultimate criterion for his theology. He must submit those needs
and insights to crucifixion and the loss of self.

A. The Loss of Self

Even though his humanity will never be annihilated, the theologian is nevertheless obliged to undergo an endless series of identity crises. Christ's total abandonement by God and man as well as his isolation in hell constitute the severest
identity crisis conceivable and yet his self is not destroyed. He rises again as a
body covered with wounds. His form appears totally shattered and yet arises with
a new splendor and new evidence. The inner-logic of his form makes this process
necessary for him and the inner-logic is the logic of love. It is this same logic that
prevents the theologian from abandoning Christ in hell. He must go the same way
with Christ. (A29 220, A45 97, A34 62, A21 237) If he is to see how Christ's form
unites God and man he must stand with Christ at the point where God's cauterizing,
wrathful holiness is fused with the pure sin of mankind. In terms of Luther's theology of the Cross he must be driven to despair by the law-giving, hidden God. (A40
58) Like the widow in the gospel he is compelled to join Christ in giving away that
which he needs to exist. He repeatedly finds himself in a position of utter helplessness, weakness and foolishness.

He must allow himself to be de-selfed so that the mid-point of his existence
and of all his psychological experiences is placed outside of himself into Christ and
the Christian community. (A30 209, W&G I 239, A12 246f, A34 81) Only if he is
willing to be stripped of his own values and of control over himself as well as any
rights to rewards or consolations for himself, can he finally be rid of all false gods
and opened to receive the true God. (A46 181, A12 145, A14 332) He must be as radical with himself as the religions were that practiced human sacrifice. (A29 375,
A46 501f) The self is no longer a home, a ground, a justification or a source of reliance; these must be sought elsewhere. (A30 248f, W&G I 214ff, 239) Christ's
beauty robs him of the time and inclination to be concerned about the fulfillment of
any needs or desires that he may discover in himself. (A12 219, A46 129, A30 238,
A46 475) His basic movement is not deeper into the self but away from it towards
another. (W&G II 298f) Although he comes to know himself in this movement and only
here, he cannot stop to reflect on himself without impeding the flight of love he is
caught up in. If he does, he will inevitably begin to sink like Peter. (A15 88, A30
228) He must let go of himself and not try to keep turning back to be sure he is having the experience of love and faith or to reassure himself against despair and
temptation. (A40 88, W&G I 204f, 241) The gospels make it clear that the self and

its realization is to be forgotten, left behind and hated. (A29 107) The Christian is an actor taken up in his role, the deed to be done, and forgetful of himself, the doer. (B9 84f)

B. The Loss of Understanding

This experience of a profound identity crisis or loss of self is what lies at the basis of all dialectical theology from Abelard to Luther to Hegel to Barth. It focuses its primary attention on the discontinuity of understanding. New understanding comes only with the loss of previous understanding. Protestant dialectical theology, as discussed above (cf. supra, pp. 41ff) focuses on the scandal of Christ.

Despite Balthasar's rigorous criticism of dialectical theology and his emphasis on the analogy of Being, he has given frequent testimony to the fundamental influence of Karl Barth on his theology. (A14, A44 6ff, A28 5-159) Kierkegaard, the theologian of paradox, was also one of the earliest and most abiding influences. (A44 12, 22) He is fully aware of the necessity for the attacks by Luther, Kierkegaard and Barth on Catholicism and liberalism. He shares their fundamental concern over the loss of the specifically Christian substance: the unification of the cross and resurrection, the union of life and death in Christ's form. What unites the cross and resurrection is Christ's descent into the hell of human sin and isolation. For Christ himself this is a moment of total discontinuity when the universe loses its transparency to the Absolute and his past life seems meaningless. No analogy of any kind can find its way into this moment. Christ's theology, therefore, is dialectical, but Christian theology is not. Because the Christian descends into hell only in the company of Christ and is not abandoned by Christ even in the lowest circle of hell, he does not experience a total discontinuity between death and life, between earth and heaven. Christ is a continuous bridge uniting the two. Christ is paradoxically both sinner and justified at the same time. The Christian, however, experiences a continuous movement from his sin to his justification.

Nevertheless, this continuity is by no means smooth and easy to understand. The loss of self in order to find a new self implies a loss of understanding to find a new one. The theologian must be prepared to encounter the form of Christ repeatedly as a scandal, and to see in the scandal a proof of Christ's uniqueness and transcendence. The scandal of Christ lies in the theologian's inability to place Jesus in any classification. He can find no rational, sensible explanation for the development of Christ's form. The closer he comes to Christ, the more convinced he is that not even the greatest of religious geniuses could have created Christ's form, much less the obscure authors of the New Testament. No one but the Spirit could have put into his form the perfect balance between humility to the point of abjection and majesty to the point of divinization. (A40 64, A30 165, A28 59, A30 452) No one but God could have united death and life so intimately in one form.

No philosophy or religion could foresee the manifestation of the greatest conceivable divine and human splendor precisely in the supreme humiliation of death. The cross of Christ is anything but a synthesis of what philosophy and religion consider the most exalted in God and man. (A30 470) It is rather the encounter of God and man in their weakest, most helpless and impoverished states. No philosophic or religious synthesis would have the authority to make death the mid-point of a unique, personal, eternal existence; none could offer man that kind of life by demanding that he stop seeking it and lose it. (A39 20f, A29 370, A46 75, 77) None could call the believer to see success in obvious failure. Only Christ can credibly call man to sacrifice himself together with a crucified Jew for the sake of a God who deserts that Jew and of a fellow man who persecutes him. (A46 498, A30 648) The Christian is called to exist in the event of Christ's death and resurrection, in the timeless, placeless hell of Holy Saturday between the crucifixion with Christ in baptism and the final resurrection with Christ in the parousia. (B132 349, A39 13, 42) No immanent evolution, no human effort, insight, hope or love can mediate between the eternal death of Good Friday and the eternal life of Easter. Only the solitude and silence of God's death on Holy Saturday can bridge that abyss. (A45 39, 131) This means for the Christian that his existence is an encounter with a consuming fire which is objectively the resurrection of a unique person but is experienced subjectively as crucifixion. It appears to the non-believer as a meaningless, fruitless self-annihilation. (A12 131f, A32 500f, A16 87)

Anyone, therefore, who sees Jesus as merely a prophet and interprets the descent to hell, the resurrection, the Incarnation and the Trinity as inventions of the early Church will have to interpret Christianity as placing all human existence under the law of death, as denying all life and destroying all human logic. (A34 56, A45 60) On the basis of human logic no one could synthesize a form that identifies the eternal life of the unique person with death. Death cannot be made the very form of such a life. (A39 119ff, B8 52, A29 373, 2 Cor. 6:9) Greek tragedy comes closest to making death a sacrament of such life but ultimately loses faith. (A32 766, A36 119) Not even the myths about ascending and descending gods dared to see in the death of the god more than a blow of fate that the god must endure. Only in Christianity is death itself salvific, the source of life and the definitive expression of divine life. (A30 485)

Because Jesus does claim that he and he alone expresses supreme divine power in the helplessness of human death, he is a scandal for human logic. (A45 187) On the basis of all human evidence it is absurd to believe that God is triune, self-sufficient love who nevertheless assumes human form and endures death and desolation for the sake of a few humans on a tiny little particle of dust in a vast universe. (A32 578, A40 65) As long as reason refuses to be transcended by faith, all that the Christian sees as balance and proportion in Christ's form appears to it as contradiction. (A46 204ff, A30 460ff) That God could be so wasteful with his love, pour it out into such hatred and endure such contradiction is credible only on the basis of the evidence revealed in Christ's form. (A34 67, A30 500) That the verification of this wasteful love should in fact depend totally on the vision of a unique, historical form is a further contradiction for reason, since that dependence appears to limit reason's openness. Moreover, if the cross really is a portrayal of divine love mutilated by human sin, it is an all too powerful manifestation of man's baseness. If man is to maintain any degree of self-esteem, he must deny that such love is possible. (A30 502, A46 302, 354) Such love threatens the psychological-sociological order that man has created. (B102 19) It turns all human wisdom into foolishness and demands a much more radical rejection of knowledge than even Socrates could call for. (A32 606, 618, A39 21) Such love shatters all man's notions of justice, proportion, balance and love only to demand from him a decidedly "unjust," "unreasonable" love that vastly overburdens him. (A30 194, A40 63, A44 13, C25)

This scandalous yet credible interpretation of death that emerges from the New Testament shows that such Christology must have been inspired by the historical Jesus. The inspiration could not come from the unbridled enthusiasm of the New Testament authors, because the proportion between the teaching and existence of Jesus is too perfect and the calm and sobriety of scripture is too profound. Likewise the ease and gracefulness with which Jesus unites and fulfils a multitude of Old Testament figures shows that the inspiration could not be derived from a painstaking, belabored attempt to convert the Jews. (A30 614ff, A45 138ff) On their own inspiration the New Testament authors could not have planted the seeds that led to such a scandalous yet convincing Christology. The evangelists would have required a much more highly developed understanding of Christology than they had if their gospels were trying to marshal evidence in support of such a Christology. They would have had to invent a teaching for Christ that was incomprehensible before his death and resurrection yet comprehensible afterwards. Their imaginations cannot account for the power and splendor that Christ's form has had over the centuries. (A30 452, 469, 485, A40 65)

Therefore, if the theologian is to understand Christ, he must allow himself to be stripped of his pre-understanding and look at the form of Christ in the light of its own evidence. The new evidence is like a powerful blinding light that both obscures any former light he had and through its brightness fills him with darkness. Most of the new evidence is at first incomprehensible and unuseable. It is not a light he can use to answer his old questions or solve his old problems but a light that uses him to answer its questions and solve its problems. In Ebeling's words, he knows himself surrendered to an unknowable, uncontrollable future; he is robbed of all security and serving an event that lies beyond his control. (W&G II 13, 167, 302, 395, G&W 44f, 61, 88f, T&V 99f) Ebeling calls this driving, expropriating force with Luther the "third use of the law. (W&G II 299) (45) It drives the theologian where he did not expect to go, does not want to go and sees no reason for going, i.e. to hell. (A30 183, 476, A44 28, A40 294) He goes because Christ goes. He cannot resist the splendor of Christ's form even when it seems to bring suicide rather than salvation. (A30 217)

He has to be persuaded more by what he does not know, see or feel than by what he does. The incomprehensible must always remain the ground and measure of the comprehensible, drawing him continually away from his own light into the ever greater night. (C4 138f) The weight of divine splendor in Christ outweighs any objections that he can make, compelling him to affirm a priori whatever radiates from

---

(45) Ebeling, "Cognitio Dei et hominis" in Geist und Geschichte der Reformation, Festschrift fuer Rueckert, AKG 38, 1966, p. 301.

Christ's form simply because it is his. (A27 34f, A39 21, A33 116, A40 63, 240, 332, A34 58, 84, A14 94f) What is his is irresistible.

Such a mode of verification makes it possible to avoid both the anthropological reduction of Bultmann and the extrinsic, positivistic verification of Barth. One has both objective and subjective analogies yet is not bound to the analogue as a norm, measure or criterion. God can verify himself without having to conform to man's expectations. He can demand what he wants when he wants without being bound by the insights of reason or the laws of nature. (A21 18) A continuity does exist between philosophy and theology but it is grounded primarily in the objective evidence. This evidence is irresistible even though it always eludes his control, largely eludes his comprehension and rarely seems to fulfil his expectations.

Chapter Four

THE MISSION OF THEOLOGY

Anima Ecclesiastica

This expropriation of the theologian's self and his understanding is part of his conformation to Christ's mission. Because the mission of Christ cannot be accomplished without the free consent of every human being at every moment of time, Christ's existence implies the church as the realization of his splendor throughout history. Because his perfect obedience conforms his subjectivity to his mission, the church as the fullness of his mission is included in his subjectivity. (A29 78) Thus Christology is impossible without ecclesiology. Christ depends on the church as his body and bride, as the completion of his faith and of his Incarnation throughout time. This makes the church the actual happening here and now of the word-event that Christ is and thereby the appearance of his fullness of power. (T&V 96ff) As the re-presentation of his form, presence and action, she is the beginning of the universe's conformation to Christ. (46)

If the theologian is to understand Christ's form, therefore, he must know himself expropriated into the fullness of Christ's form, i.e. into the church. His aesthetic sensitivity must become communized if he is to perceive the form and splendor of Christ. He must become an "anima ecclesiastica," a "communized soul."

Because Mary is the perfect recipient of revelation, she was regarded by the Fathers as the perfect "communized soul." The womb of her faith makes the Incarnation and the birth of every Christian possible. Her faith is the canonic personal center of the church giving it more than a merely physical or moral unity. She is the second Eve born from the rib of the second Adam and destined ultimately to be reunited with him. (A46 83ff, 418, A47 35, 138, A29 21f) By the grace of the crucifixion and resurrection she has been enabled to affirm unconditionally and a priori the fullness of revelation. Without such a recipient revelation would be restricted and the response of creation limited. Mary's faith opens to the whole of creation access to the eschatological reconciliation of all things. (A47 138ff, A46 85)

The theologian seeking to understand Christ's form, therefore, must sink himself into Mary's faith as the personal nucleus of the church. He must allow himself to be expropriated into Christ's mission the same way she was. Just as she was ultimately forced by Christ on the cross to sacrifice her motherly affection, so too the theologian cannot expect to bring his affections and concerns about others along as criteria for Christian understanding. He cannot cling to his political and social

---

(46) Barth, Karl, Kirchliche Dogmatik IV/2, p. 680

concerns and accept or reject Christ's revelation as it seems to answer them. (A39 26ff) He cannot simply use Christ's Trinitarian splendor to promote social welfare nor can he worship the Trinity primarily in order to save man. The theologian must allow himself to be stripped of these concerns initially so that he can clearly acknowledge the primacy of the religious act as such. (A39 87ff) The uses of God's beauty must be initially forgotten in order simply to celebrate it.

Having thus initially been robbed of his concern both for his own salvation and that of others, he shares in Christ's love for the Father. This love leads him immediately, as it led Christ, to a new concern for his brother. Worshipping the Father he comes to know his fellow man as one for whom God has died, for whom God has assumed all guilt and endured final judgement. In Christ, therefore, and only in Christ does the love of God become identical with the love of man and the love of man with the love of God. (A46 411, A39 95f) Because Christ's form is constituted by the love of the Father and the love of man, the theologian cannot understandingly contemplate Christ's form and splendor without practicing this unified love. The Christian contemplative cannot leave the world to meditate on the splendor of God without coming to understand his contemplative life as lived for the sake of the world. (A19, A40 315, A41 229ff, A46 428, A32 515f) The theologian sees his brother in God and in responding to God he cannot be drawn away from his brother in any ultimate way. Even when the vision of God leads to the hatred of parents, relatives and friends that Jesus spoke of, it still evokes a love that hates only in order to save. All fraternal love, therefore, is grounded in the vision of God's love for man, in the vision of the Father sending the Son into the depths of the human situation. The theologian should be so caught up in Christ's desire to carry out the Father's will to save man, that even without explicit reflection on the Father, the theologian is aware of the Father whenever he looks at his brother. (A46 418) Ebeling, therefore, is showing an inadequate understanding of this union between God and man when he insists that one love his neighbor not because of God but because of the neighbor's need. (W&G II 21) Loving one's brother because it is God's will in no way implies that one is insensitive to the brother's need and right to be loved. On the contrary, God has so sunk himself into every situation of every brother that loving God draws one even deeper into the brother's situation.

The more thoroughly the theologian allows himself to be drawn into the situation of his brother, the more thoroughly he is emersed in the relation between Christ and his bride. As this happens and he begins to identify more and more his concerns with those of the bride, his understanding will grow in objectivity. He will be absorbed into the universal perspective of the church which is epitomized by Mary's perfect receptivity to God and limitless solidarity with man. Allowing himself to be expropriated into this universal perspective means the continual self-transcendence and expansion of his intimate personal perspective to include more and more. (A30 518, A32 814ff, A33 163ff, A47 55) Paul and Pascal having been accused of heresy, both clearly showed this willingness to expand their own particular perspectives in order to share the universal perspective of the church. (A32 593, A30 534, B159 195f) Every theologian can do this the more completely he sees himself integrated into the object of his science, i.e. into the love between Christ and his bride. Such integration is the source of objectivity in his science. (A46 420)

Sharing in the mind of the church he shares in the unfolding self-understanding of Christ, who throughout history gathers all perspectives to his own. (A14 343f, A32 308)

Sharing Christ's consciousness in the search for objective understanding involves ultimately descending with him into the hells inhabited by all men. He must allow his own anxiety to flow into that of others in an attempt to alleviate them of it. He must join Christ in absorbing into himself the poison that infects others. Like Moses, Jeremias and the Suffering Servant he must stand before God as a representative of his people and allow himself for their sakes to be sundered from his closeness to God. This will mean being plunged with Christ into the experience of desolation that the sin of his people necessarily involves. (A41 174ff, A45 54) Like the prophets he must allow every aspect of his personal existence to be used for this purpose. He must strive to lay bare everything for community use, to the extent of allowing himself to be de-personalized into a function of the church. (A32 114, A30 328) His personality becomes identical with his unique share in the mission of Christ. (T&V 102, A30 342)

Paul portrays this absorption of the "I" into Christ and thus into the church by continually including in his own "I" the communities he has founded. (A29 176f) He refers to the perils and trials of his missionary journies as proofs of his solidarity with their pain. Not even the most damnable action of his communities exists outside his "I" because he is even willing to be damned for their sakes. (A45 57f, A32 807) He cries over their sinfulness as if it were his own. Because of his conformation to Christ, however, not even this pain and love are his; they are Christ's pain and Christ's love. Thus his heart becomes the heart of the church and he becomes the epitomy of the church. (A29 180, 382, A32 339f)

To the extent a theologian is able thus to lose himself through boundless solidarity with others, he will find himself anew and help others to find their new selves. As he is thus expropriated into the church and assists in the rebirth of others, this discovery of his own new self and of his midwifery will give him a deeper understanding of the triumph of love over death. As the threat of death, the ultimate enemy of love, is removed, he will discover in himself a vast new freedom to love. He is freed from the fear that any love relationship will be buried in a mound of guilt and ultimately annihilated by death. (A34 77f) He is no longer compelled to seek manipulative power or subservience as a way of dealing with this threat. (A47 144) Knowing himself and his brother to be embraced by the death-conquering love of the Trinity, he is given the right to a profound new trust in himself and his brother, to a new hope for their love. (A40 303, A46 429)

The Transparency of the Object

Having seen the object of theology and been expropriated by it into the "communized soul," the theologian is suited to take up his task of keeping the church transparent for all men to the splendor of Christ.

The church is transparent when it is composed of Christians who are willing with Christ and in Christ to love to the end. She shows this willingness by abandoning the pursuit of her own form and splendor. She must see that she has no figure, splendor, ideas or plans of her own but is called upon to become clay in which the Spirit can mold the form of Christ. By not resisting the guidance of the Spirit, the form and splendor of Christ can become visible in the structures of the institutional church. It is this transparency that unifies the church and gives her credibility. (A30 538ff, 206) Because Christ has made the appearance of the Father's love in himself dependent on the witness of Christian lives he depends on this transparency of the church. (W&G I 251)(47) The church must manifest the hypostatic union between God and man and the Trinitarian union among the persons of God. This is the beauty of Christ that she concretizes and the incense that she emits. (A36 977ff) She hands down the very person of Jesus; he is the content of her tradition, the gospel in person. (A32 752) She is the representation and form of Christ's presence and action; she is the continuation of the word-event that Christ is. He appears in the scriptures, in the holiness of the church's members, in her infallible teaching, in her ritual and in her institutional structures. Every aspect of the church should be transparent to his splendor and reducible to his form. (A30 548, 519, 205) Therefore, everything about her is sacramental and all her actions have the same structure as her specifically designated sacraments. (A30 243, A46 497, A40 218)

Serving as mankind's access and response to the form of Christ, the church belongs to both the object and to the act of theology. Because no word of address is complete without the response it evokes, the church in her response to God's word is a part of that word and therefore a part of theology's object. (A46 511, A30 191ff, 296) The object of theology embraces the total form of Christ, both head and body, both groom and bride. (A30 506) The church belongs to this form, however, only as a passing witness who is constantly striving to eliminate herself. She longs for the day when she will become co-exstensive with the universe and "wither away." She is merely a momentary instrument of the Spirit as he works for the salvation of the universe.

She is not in any way an intermediary or "go-between" that separates God and man but the place where God and man unite. (A30 209f) Even Christ cannot be called a mediator in the Old Testament sense because he actually is the presence of God. Having been liquified in the eucharist and placed immediately into the hands of sinners, Christ is more than a mediator. (A46 139) The church must strive, therefore, never to interfere with this immediacy. She must recognize her own inadequacy and with Peter and Paul weep over all the disfigurements of Christ's image that abound in her. (A30 544) Her opaqueness is often more a scandal than her transparency is a witness. She must also realize how ridiculous and hypocritical her actual achievements make her look in the face of her exalted aspirations. This is the inevitable tragedy of her situation, yet even this weakness is an opportunity for her to share the

---

(47) Ebeling, Vom Gebet, p. 60.

humiliation and lowliness of her head and groom. Just as the glory of the Trinity appears in Christ supremely on the cross, so too the church is most transparent in her humiliated foolishness, her helplessness and defenselessness. (A46 241, A29 203ff) She demands the eyes of faith in order to see her transparency and radiates only enough that the non-believer can grasp the hand extended to him in the darkness. (A30 543)

Although this transparency should be realized in all members and structures of the church, most Christians are able to reveal only the most infinitesimal portion of Christ's glory. (A32 766, T&V 81) For this reason the church is profoundly dependent on her canonized and uncanonized saints who are willing to follow Christ "to the end."

The more intensely the saint lives the evangelical counsels, the more transparent he becomes and the more the authority of the church is increased. (B54 645ff, A46 462)

Because of their special transparency the lives and writings of the saints are prime theological sources. They bring out hidden or forgotten aspects of revelation. (A12 19) and serve as lighthouses to guide the church and her theology. (A39 127) Their existence is lived theology making them normal or canonic Christians. (A12 29f) Not the average modern consciousness but the consciousness of the saints is the criterion of theology. (A32 518, A40 257f) Because they come closest to Christ's identity of life and teaching, their lives come closest to containing the fullness of the church's teaching and their teaching the fullness of the church's life. (A28 195) By looking at them above all else, theology discovers what the church truly is. (A34 82) Their light removes the guilt and darkness that obscure the true nature of the church. (A40 257f, A28 198) Nevertheless, rather than leading theology to diminish the difference between themselves and Christ, they see the difference more keenly than anyone. Precisely because of their closeness to Christ they are best able to remind theology of the difference between their light and the light of Christ in them. They know best the insignificance of their witness in comparison to the object to which they witness. (A40 35, A30 207)

In addition to the transparency of the saints and of his own existence, the theologian depends for the credibility of his theology on being able to demonstrate the appearance of Christ's splendor in the lives of all Christians. (A25 57) Since the love of Christians is the visibility of Christ and Christ is the visibility of God, God relies on the fraternal love of Christians to prove his love. (1 John 4:20f, A30 231, A46 429) The theologian, therefore, must be able to point out the whole of Christian dogmatics in the brotherly love of the church if he is to make it concrete, sensual and credible. (A30 409, A47 41) The world depends on the fruits of believers in order to see the truth of their faith; it complains about Christianity primarily because so few Christian lives come anywhere near assimilation to their words. (W&G II 50, A28 216)(48) As much higher as Christ's credibility is than the credibility of his

---

(48) Ebeling, "Die Frage nach den Früchten des Geistes" in <u>Zeitschrift fuer Theologie und Kirche</u> 1969 p. 364.

witnesses, his word does depend on all Christians to achieve its full realization and credibility in history. (A40 60, T&V 95ff)

Scripture

In its attempt to show the church's transparency theology must show that the New Testament does not offer us a first-century, Jewish-Hellenistic, mythological distortion of Jesus of Nazareth but the canonic revelation of Jesus Christ.

We spoke above of the legitimacy and necessity of knowing the objective form of Jesus Christ. The question now is whether such a knowledge is possible. Whereas the reason for denying the transparency of scripture lies in a forgetfulness of the Spirit, the consequence of denying it is the failure of Christ's mission. (A30 507, 527ff) If the Spirit cannot make divine splendor appear in scripture, Christ cannot make it appear in the whole of creation.

The historical-critical method has made it abundantly clear that scripture is not the word or sacrament of God in the same sense that Christ is but that as a part of the church it gives an essential witness to him. (A30 522) It attempts to translate the word made flesh back into a written word that is able both to be handed down through history and to maintain a continuity between the "historical Jesus" and the "Christ of Faith." (A46 140, A47 90) Scripture, however, can give only a poor reflection of the non-word, silence, supra-word that Christ became on the cross and in his descent into hell. (A40 34, A46 78) The authors had to draw on a variety of Jewish and Hellenistic traditions and present four different accounts of his life in order to come anywhere near capturing in human language his full reality. (A46 141, 145) They profoundly humilitate Jesus by giving him a written body that can be exposed to the spiritlessness of literary criticism and all the abuses of language. Yet precisely in this humiliated form scripture receives a share in the transparency of Christ's mutilated body on the cross and in the eucharist. (A30 519, A32 616f)

If the reader does not cling to the letter with philological zeal but like Mary Magdalene lets it rise, it will raise the reader into the dimension of the Spirit and spiritual understanding. (A34 70, A31 310, A40 99f) The Spirit draws the reader into the common vision of the risen Christ whence all the varying and conflicting theologies of the New Testament are derived. He draws him into a reality that vastly transcends the text. The words of the text are like the seed that must die in order to bear fruit and the bread that must be broken in order to be eaten: it must be turned and opened to reveal its full meaning. (A25 57)

But how can the Spirit reveal the full meaning of Christ in words that are rarely if ever the very words of the historical Jesus but rather statements of faith by the early church? The answer lies again in the activity of the Spirit in the composition of scripture. (A30 519) Just as the Spirit caused the word of God to be fruitful and grow in Mary's physical womb and in the womb of her faith, so too he implants the words of Jesus into the womb of faith he has formed in the apostolic church. (A19 306, A30 515) The same Spirit who dwelled in Jesus dwelled in the new church and gave it a special ability to objectively interpret Christ's past life for its new situation. (A30 331, 515, A46 141, A45 161ff) The Spirit enabled them to make the first transposition of Jesus from his own time and place into the time of the church and thereby established for her the means to make continual transpositions throughout history. (A46 143) As the first hermeneut the Spirit gave the church a norm and canon for her later hermeneutic activity. The canonic portrayal he created in scripture is richer than any objective account of the "historical Jesus," for Jesus comes to himself only within the faith that he causes. (A30 518, 394, A30 506) The faith of the church is a necessary part of the word of God and therefore all the distinctly first-century Palestinian elements in scripture have been incorporated into that word. (A28 94, 74) These passing elements show that God reveals himself by thrusting himself into the depths of the human and making it transparent. (A28 91) It becomes clear that God and not the church produce the form of scripture. The church is merely the womb in which the Spirit, calling upon the church's powers of imagination, creates the form. (A30 517) He creates it inspite of all that the authors themselves find confusing, embarassing or scandalous. (A46 144)

By thus inspiring scripture and surrendering it into the hands of the church for interpretation throughout history, the Spirit converts Christ into a universalized spiritual reality that is free, all-powerful and omnipresent. (A30 527) Because of scripture the church is able to give witness in all situations to the normative moment of her birth. (A30 524) As can be seen even within the Old and New Testaments, every time she does bring this earliest witness into a new situation, new dimensions of its meaning are opened up. Although one could not say that the church fathers had an inferior understanding of scripture than the present church, the understanding today is obviously different. The fullness of understanding in the scriptures, guarantees that this change in understanding will not involve a major shift in emphasis or proportion. (A30 531) The change will not be a distortion as long as the interpreter maintains a deep sensitivity to the supreme interpreter, the Spirit. The Spirit gives the interpreter freedom to create new tradition, as is especially obvious in the writings of the patristic and medieval writers. Our contemporary philological exegete often fails to appreciate the profound, poetic unified richness of their "allegorical exegesis" in his all too timid, Spiritless clinging to the literal, historical and "existential" meanings. (A40 99ff) In the single events of scripture he must learn to see the fullness of revelation and thus a multitude of interpretations. Only in this way can the Spirit reveal to him the Christological meaning and spirit of each passage for each individual in each unique situation. (A30 527ff) In Hamann's words "The literal, grammatical and historical meaning are mystical to the fullest extent and without ascending to heaven the interpreter cannot acquire the key to their meaning." (A32 635)

Sacraments

Scripture like all theology is a sacramental reality that precedes all the particular sacraments; it is a necessary precondition for the interior action of grace. (A25 98) The two testaments are the breasts of the church by which Christ feeds the world, vehicles by which he actualizes the form of revelation into effective grace. (A25 57, 98, A30 526) The Spirit creates history with the sacrament of scripture by transforming the world and making it transparent. (A25 76, A30 509) It has this power because, like the eucharist, it is an aspect of Christ's body.

Although the specific sacraments play a subordinate role to the sacramentality of scripture and the preaching of the word they do have the identical function. (A30 577f) This identity appears in the dependence of preaching and scripture on the unique presence of the "Christ of faith" at the eucharistic celebration. The function of all the sacraments is to make the "Christ of faith" perceptible throughout history. (A30 508) They do this not by virtue of their own form but through their participation in Christ's form. (A30 560)

The eucharist makes present to the community the heart of Christ's form: his total self-surrender to the Father for the sake of humanity. This sacrifice is the church's inner form around which her whole life is centered. (A46 91, A45 68, A30 523ff) Her basic task of bodily expressing Christ's love happens clearly here where flesh speaks to flesh, (A30 388, 553) and bride and groom meet to enter a physical communion. (A30 551f) Matrimony also re-presents this beauty of the marriage between Christ and the church and draws all marriages into the church's transparency. (A30 554, A25 109) Penance is perhaps the clearest model for all the sacraments in that the priest's love, forgiveness and reception into the community are transparent to God's love, forgiveness and reception. (A30 558) Penance shows the crucial importance of conscious perception and free decision,---something that infant baptism tends to badly obscure. (A30 557) All of the sacraments are clearly intended to render man transparent to Christ's splendor by sinking Christ's form into man. Christ is the form and man is the matter of all sacraments. (A30 561, A46 285)

Institution

The theologian must make it clear that the authority of the institutional church depends on its transparency to the splendor of Christ and its transparency rests in its holiness. (A32 178f, 181, 199ff, 262f, A20 234ff, A28 161ff, 196ff, A54) A church official is valueless to the extent that he resembles the depersonalized functionary of the modern state. Unless he can be seen to have conformed himself to Christ's radical obedience to the Father on the cross, he will be unable to radiate the weight of divine splendor, his sole means of evoking reverence and obedience. (A46 89, A30 203ff, 337ff, 537ff, 575) He exists solely to serve the holiness of the church by drawing its members into the form of Christ. (B76 305) His power to do so lies like Christ's power in his poverty, weakness and humiliation. (A29 424ff, A46 160) By means of them he makes Christ's power present and disregards his own power. (B159 196, A33 143) He is legitimized by the surrendering of his life for his sheep. (A30 575ff) Like Peter any man must be terrified to accept an ecclesial office and like Paul every Christian must be willing to endure the scandal of an institution that cannot bear the enormous burden placed upon it. (A40 362, A30 544ff, B74 622) This sinfulness of the hierarchy will constantly force the hierarchy to borrow its lacking love from the church of love, as Peter did from John. (A34 79f, John 21) It will remind the hierarchy that it exists only as a channel to pass on that love, that it is only a means whereas the life of the church is the goal. (A29 427, A32 204f, A30 206) It will prevent the hierarchy from forgetting that not it but Christ is the shepherd. (A29 428)

Doctrine

Along with scripture, the saints, the sacraments and the hierarchy, the teaching of the church must share the church's sacramental transparency. (A30 204, 531, 579) It is one of the ways in which the event of Christ is handed down from generation to generation. (T&V 13) The sole purpose of the dogmas and their theological elaboration is to sketch the form of Jesus, to clarify and demonstrate the proportions and contours of his total existence. (A30 119) In his form is contained the whole of dogmatics and in its ability to portray that form lies the legitimacy of dogmatics. (A14 278, A47 11, A46 80) For that reason the fundamental truth of every dogma and theological treatise is the Christological dogma: Jesus is the Christ, the Son of God. The Trinitarian dogma arises only as its presupposition and the soteriological-ecclesiological doctrines as its consequence. (A30 568, A47 87) The theologian must be able to open a vision through all the corridors and back rooms of theology to this one dogma and beyond the dogma to the increasingly incomprehensible, elusive reality of Christ himself: the fidelity between God and man. (A30 562) Christ's reality is the object and motive of faith to which dogma merely witnesses. (A30 170f) The theologian must, therefore, allows dogma continually to reveal that reality. (A46 96ff, A34 70, A30 570, 203ff, W&G II 108) The theologian must allow God's most intimate expression of his heart on the cross to appear in all its splendor and irresistibility. (A40 314) He must make theology another medium for Christ to glorify himself. (A30 578) The Spirit must be allowed to draw the theologian beyond an all too timid, slavish treatment of the dogmas into the free, spontaneous creativity of the mystic. (A32 207, A34 70f, A40 242) The Spirit will show the theologian the full mystery of God hidden in the words of the church's dogma, teachers and thinkers. (A28 91) The theologian can then help to translate the words of theology into events so that others can experience there the very reality of those words.

The theologian's fusion of word and deed, of Marian holiness and Petrine teaching, re-presents the identity of holiness and doctrine that was in Christ. (A30 204) Like all the other aspects of the church, dogmatics has no form of its own but shares in Christ's form. Because the form of Christ can be revealed only by believers to believers, the theologian must of course be making statements of faith and not merely indulging in neutral speculation or historical fact finding. The light of faith must radiate from any theological statement that is to convince human reason. (A30 158, T&V 109) Each statement itself must be measured by obedience and worship if it is to effect obedience and worship in the world.

In order for theology thus to maintain this transparency for a world that is constantly in flux, it must remain in dialogue with all of its own tradition as well as with the contemporary world. Like the arts it must remain sensitive to the style of thought and experience of a particular epoch and be ready to translate its past mode of expression into a contemporary style. (A24 136f) This implies a close attention to the new saints evoked by new situations, for their lives will provide the crucial criterion for the continual reinterpretation of Christ's life. (A28 168, A27 75ff) Such awareness enables the Spirit to reveal new aspects of divine truth that could be understood only in this particular epoch. (A24 187) The sole purpose of this continual reinterpretation is to draw Christians back into the fiery furnace that is the center of all Christianity: the encounter of God and sin on the cross. (A24 187) The purpose is not to gloss over the terror of this central mystery. The new understanding always appears to shatter old forms and plummits the believer into darkness and scandal. (A27 75ff) The new dogma in turn serves only as a signpost and lighthouse on the way into the endlessness of truth. (B48 216f) In a certain sense it is even impossible to speak of a development of dogma since each traveller must set out anew. What Peguy says about philosophers applies to theologians: they do not have any disciples. (A32 18) Every theologian, therefore, must be willing to make a total criticism of what has gone before and undertake a bold new creative effort. (A40 98f, A6 viii ff) Turning anew to Jesus he must strive to assess what is right for the times insofar as those times are both determined by a certain tradition and called to assume a new responsibility for the future. (49) He must learn both to recognize contemporary aberrations along the fruitless paths of past heretical movements as well as to remind the Church that her theology is semper reformanda and can remain faithful to its truest self only by constantly changing. (B18 83f) Scripture will remain the norm for this change but it will be normative only as it is read within the church together with all who have ever read it. (W&G II 211) Just as the scriptures are themselves a continual speaking of the word of God into new situations, the dogmas must unfold and integrate themselves into every new situation. (G&W 75, A41 346ff, A36 20) Not the letter alone but the Spirit of the letter of scripture is the norm of tradition that allows scripture to renew itself, to creatively open up whole new worlds. (G&W 76, A30 569)

This creation of new worlds is after all the function of the church, and theology makes its contribution to the church by elaborating the conditions for the possibility of creating a new way of life. (A34 75) By constantly placing before the church's eyes the form and measure of Christ, it aids the Spirit to conform the church and thereby the world to Christ. (A29 130, A28 162, A30 578) By representing the church's belief in Christ, it gives the world certitude and salvation. (W&G II 67, 205) As Dante's theology demonstrated perhaps best of all, it can become the norm for a living culture. (A32 371)

Eschatological Reduction

Insofar as theology and the other ecclesial media do become norms of culture, they are on their way towards self-elimination. (A30 509) By conforming the whole of culture to Christ's form they will make all the forms of nature that lead up to man and all the forms that man creates transparent to the Trinitarian splendor of Christ. (A25 96, B13 44) Through the church Christ, the Alpha and the Omega of creation, will

---

(49) Ebeling, "Der Theologe und sein Amt," in Zeitschrift fuer Theologie und Kirche 66, 1969, p. 250.

turn the entire universe into a sacrament of his presence so that the specific medium of the church is no longer necessary. The entire universe will be drawn into the liturgical act that is Christ. The old passes away in its fiery judgement and all will be made new: a new heaven and a new earth. (A36 654ff) The world will be transformed into a theophany in that all forms will be hypostatically united with the form of Christ. Through the Spirit's activity in the church Christ will be revealed as the head of the universe and the universe will appear as the body of Christ. (A28 214, A30 653) The entire universe, every person in every situation, will speak of Christ because he is the only proper measure and proportion between heaven and earth. (A24 222, A29 375f, A30 209, T&V 81) Christian revelation will be fully interpreted. (A30 91) World history will copy the church's history; the relation between Christ and the church will become the measure of all historical situations. (A27 112) The universe will become the realization of the perfect man, Christ. (A30 537)

In having served the Spirit to make the world transparent to Christ, theology will have reached its highest fulfillment and its first activity: the glorification of the Father. (A28 162, 222) Worship is the beginning, the end and the abiding measure of theology. Dionysius the Areopagite portrays theology as the ordering of heaven, earth, men and angels around the throne of God joined in a hymn of praise. (A32 176f, 157) Peguy's theology culminates repeatedly in prayer, in a noble playing before God. (A32 835, 870f) Theology must see its intellectual pursuit as an attempt to praise, glorify and thank God and only secondarily as kerygma and dialogue. (A47 57, 62) Only as the theology of praise can it allow God to be God. (50) Only a praying theology can see the God of scripture because in scripture God is above all else a God to be worshipped. (A46 249) The theologian, therefore, is continually forced with the seraphim to cover his eyes before the object of his science: the splendor of Christ's love. Its brightness is such that it can be seen only through blind adoration. (A10 312) In order to understand he must be drawn beyond the realm of the word into the wordless realm of the Spirit. (A40 295) His theology must exhaust itself in dumbstruck worship before the appearance of God's inscrutable splendor. (A32 173)

---

(50) Ebeling, Luther, p. 298.
   Ebeling, "Das Verständnis vom Heil in einer sekularisierten Zeit," in Kontexte IV, ed. H.J. Schultz, 1967, p. 13

The greatest significance of Balthasar's theological method lies in his incorporation into systematic theology of literary sources and of the sources traditionally handled by spiritual and mystical theology. In so doing he exhibits an important proximity to Marechal and to the many contemporary Catholic theologians who stand on his shoulders. He shares with them and the existentialist theologians of Protestantism their radical critique of conceptualism, rationalism and historicism by developing with them the decisive importance of feeling and decision in the process of understanding. Where he differs from most contemporary theologians is in his appreciation for the centrality of form and the permanent necessity of symbols to maintain the credibility of any form. This appreciation of form and symbol leads him, along with the Protestant neo-orthodox theologians, to an insistence on the uniqueness and otherness of Christ's form and on the inevitably scandalous character of the evidence that it contains. This scandal in turn demands intense, continual self-denial on the part of the theologian if he is to perceive that evidence. Balthasar's greatest value to Christianity as a whole lies perhaps here in his persistent uncomfortable reminder that the true Christian, and in a special way the true Christian theologian, will always be a scandal to the majority and a potential martyr.

This strength is rooted in the apocalyptic spirit that pervades his theology. It is the dependence of this apocalyptic spirit on the continual maintenance of a state of crisis that provides the key to the greatest weakness in his theology.

Due to the apocalyptic origins of Christianity this is a weakness that has plagued a great deal of Christian theology. It has been especially evident during periods of profound social upheavel such as the collapse of the Roman Empire and the disintegration of medieval culture. Balthasar's apocalypticism emerges most clearly in his emphasis on the cross and his designation of the uniqueness of Christianity as its offering of life in death and not after death. (cf. supra p. 59, 75) Along with the early theology of Protestant neo-orthodoxy his theology deserves the title, "Theology of Crisis." He firmly believes that man finds his greatest fulfillment in being put to the test, in enduring the severest possible ordeals. This appreciation of the state of crisis may well arise largely out of a strong experience of what social scientists refer to as "disaster utopia" or "disaster euphoria."(51) It occurs shortly after the greatest impact of a disaster and is a "great upsurge of goodwill among the survivors and on the part of the outsiders who come to their aid." (52) It is largely upon such an experience that apocalyptic religions base their hope

---

(51) Michael Barkun, Disaster and the Millenium, New Haven and London, Yale University Press, 1974, p. 163f

(52) Barkum, Ibid.

that the impending disaster will begin a radical transformation of society. When one considers that Balthasar spent his childhood in Switzerland during World War I and published his first book, The Apocalypse of the German Soul, while living in Munich during the 1930's and in Basel during the war, it is easy to understand why as sensitive a theologian as he would be drawn to a "theology of the cross" or a "theology of crisis." It is also understandable that he would be attracted to people like Claudel, Bernanos, Peguy, Dostoyevsky, Ignatius of Loyola, Augustine and John the Evangelist who all underwent profound personal crises and/or participated intimately in the profound social crises of their times. He shares with them a deep mistrust of man's attempts to create and control his own life in the pursuit of stability and security.

A study of the dynamic of apocalyptic religion and its dependence on a continual state of crisis reveals the major characteristics of Balthasar's theology and the dynamic that underlies it. According to Barkun apocalyptic movements are evoked by a severe disaster or series of disasters. If a crisis is so severe that it shakes the foundations of a culture, it leaves the individual feeling overwhelmed by his own helplessness and compelled to look outside of himself to "the other" for salvation. It seems essential to survival that everyone demonstrate profound solidarity with the misery of their fellow victims and that all find their strength primarily in the charisma, beauty and power of a great leader-savior-messias. The all important virtues are steadfast compassion and the ability to contemplate, celebrate and obey the splendor of the savior.

As Eric Neumann has demonstrated, such a crisis is usually accompanied by the emergence of the "shadow," i.e. a complex composed of all the "unacceptable" feelings that the individual and the group had been repressing before the crisis. (53) The terrifying emergence of the shadow evokes on the one hand an aspiration to the highest conceivable ideals represented by the savior and a rejection of all the values of the old culture and on the other hand a reduction of man to his most basic instincts Christianity in its apocalyptic forms usually opts initially for the former but often culminates eventually like Nazism in a fusion of the two. Both of these inflationary and deflationary reactions to a crisis, however, fail to face the real problem which is the integration of the shadow into man's consciousness. While the inflationary reaction dominates, one pursues with intense enthusiasm the ideals of the savior and flees with equal enthusiasm the primitive instincts of the shadow. Because such an idealist feels continually threatened by the instinctual and in flight above the abyss, he identifies the self with the instinctual and makes asceticism, self-denial and self-sacrifice the center of his ethics. Thus great emphasis is placed on the self-sacrificing, vicarious suffering of the savior and on the selflessness of a God who has no nee to create but does so out of the pure graciousness of His being. Such a theology of crisis will exhort people to seek union with God by becoming as needless as He through total self-surrender and a priori affirmation of a savior's demands. Poverty chastity and obedience become the primary expressions of this selfless love. They

---

(53) Depth Psychology and a New Ethic, New York, Harper & Row, 1973, pp. 85ff

are denials of man's instinctual desires for material security, sensual pleasure and the power to control and create his own life. Such desires are looked upon as selfish, egotistical drives which, if yielded to in any way, could turn a state of crisis into a state of total chaos. For a theology of crisis, therefore, they are anathema. They are mistrusted as the seeds of man's attempts to satisfy himself and defy divine authority by attaining a stable, secure mastery of his own life. The past crisis is taken as a proof of the perfidity and futility of such attempts and as a presage of the impending crisis that will destroy such a Promethean culture. Apocalyptic religion, therefore, rejects contemporary culture, abandons hope of man evolving or gradually improving society and awaits in a basically receptive posture the saving powers of the messias.

Such an ethic and religion make sense within the context of a sufficiently severe crisis. Outside of that context, however, they appear to be either innocuous piety or else highly oppressive to human development. Nietzsche saw them as oppressive when he attacked Christianity for its doctrine of a needless, perfect and therefore life-denying God, as well as for its glorification of obedience. Marx rejected its oppressiveness when he attacked Christianity's static, other-worldly God and its glorification of poverty. Freud saw it when he attacked Christianity's patriarchal God and its glorification of chastity. Perhaps nothing accounts for the weakness and unpopularity of Balthasar's theology more than his almost consistent refusal to take these critiques seriously and to confront the evidence offered. He prefers instead to glory in the scandal that such a theology causes and to regard the scandal as a verification of Christianity. The theologians who seek to take these critiques seriously and to re-examine Christianity fundamentally he attacks for performing an "anthropological reduction." He criticizes such thinkers for watering Christianity down to fulfill the ordinary, instinctual needs of man. He attacks them for not being able to endure the scandal of Christianity and for not offering a true alternative to the contemporary philosophies, psychologies and sociologies that do take these critiques seriously.

When one considers analyzes of Nazism by such thinkers as Eric Neumann and Gert Kalow it seems especially urgent in our nuclear age on our extremely interdependent globe that Christian theologians take these critiques seriously.(54) Writing shortly after World War II as a German Jewish psychiatrist of the Jungian school, Neumann places the responsibility for Nazism largely at the feet of what he defines as the "old ethic." The essential characteristic of the old ethic is that it deals with evil primarily by means of suppression and repression. It disposes of

---

(54) Eric Neumann, ibid. and "Mass Man and the Phenomena of Recollectivization" in The Origins and History of Consciousness, Princeton University Press, 1954, pp. 436ff
Gert Kalow, Hitler, Das gesamtdeutsche Trauma, Muenchen, Piper Verlag, 1967

unacceptable desires by consciously or unconsciously denying their existence. It is these repressed feelings that constitute the shadow and it is the shadow that errupts violently in Nazism. Neumann believes that it is of paramount importance that one consider the impact on the unconscious of one's ethical exhortations. If one exhorts another to excessively high ideals too soon, it will result in the vigorous repression of all the feelings that do not conform to those ideals. It seems to me that Balthasar's exhortation to the highest ideals conceivable will usually have precisely this effect.

He should, therefore, be much more mindful of the danger that he will intensify man's estrangement from his basic needs, cause these needs to grow cancerously in the unconscious and leave people even more susceptible to domination by their shadows.

Theologians should carefully evaluate the strengths and weaknesses of Christianity's inherent apocalypticism. Such a reassessment would focus on the necessity of integrating the shadow into the consciousness of the Christian instead of attempting to deny its existence. Theologians should begin by joining the social scientists in taking a much closer look at the ordinary feelings of ordinary people and especially at the feelings that have been traditionally unacceptable to Christianity. They can then begin to plot with much more care the stages of individual and social development that seem to be necessary to attain the exceedingly lofty ideals of Christianity. Although we cannot forget that the Spirit blows where it will, we must be very careful not to demand that the Spirit always function drastically in a state of crisis. One need not be in a continual state of crisis in order to be a good Christian. There do seem to be patterns of gradual ethical and religious development that should ordinarily be followed step by step. Although theology cannot enslave itself to any particular theory of individual or social development, it must show a reverence for these patterns. Psychologists like Eric Neumann and Erik Erickson recognize, like Balthasar, the necessity of radical crises and conversions that are painful and precarious. However, they are opposed to the attempt typical of Christianity and especially of Balthasar's thought to see crisis as a permanent state between the lost selflessness of childhood and the unachievable selflessness of sainthood. Heeding the critiques of Nietzsche, Marx and Freud, they insist on an intermediate stage of aggressive self-assertion and self-centeredness that is profoundly sexual.(55)

Balthasar's implicit rejection of this "selfish," "egotistical" stage and his exaltation of the innocence of past childhood and future sainthood are typical of apocalyptic religions. Christianity must come to an honest affirmation of the indispensable value of the self-centered feelings and passions that seek expression during

_____

(55) Eric Neumann, "Mystical Man" in The Mystic Vision, Papers from Eranos Yearbook 6, New York and London, 1969
Erik Erickson, "Allness or Nothingness" in Young Man Luther, New York, Norton, 1958, pp. 98ff.

this middle stage. It must encourage people in the straightforward expression of anger, aggression, sexual desire and pride as well as receptivity and self-sacrifice. Christians must come to recognize in their basic needs and passions a source of divine inspiration and the roots of their own creativity. Such a recognition would enable Christianity to begin to overcome its most painful scandals: hypocrisy, reactionary theological and political stands, crusades, inquisitions, religious wars and the support of fascist regimes. Continuing to exhort people onesidedly and indiscriminately to poverty, chastity and obedience and to the search for salvation outside of themselves in "the other" will only contribute to the recurrence of such violent eruptions of repressed emotions in the future.

The supreme question that this insight poses for the Christian theologian concerns the wisdom of proclaiming a needless God and a self-sacrificing savior to people in the middle stage of development whose ultimate concern is and should be the aggressive egotistical satisfaction of deep personal needs. Do such a God and such a savior inhibit their development and is a person correct in rejecting at that time such an understanding of God and Christ? If so, might there be wisdom in working once again towards a more developmental understanding of the Trinity from which need is not excluded? Are there not times when need is ultimate and absolute? Can we learn something from the more primitive images of God in which there was struggle and conflict? Does a movement in this direction inevitably culminate in the loss of transcendence and the worship of progress as it did in the nineteenth century?

A. BIBLIOGRAPHY

I   WORKS BY VON BALTHASAR
(listed according to the numeration in A44)

A   BOOKS

1937
A1   <u>Apokalypse der deutschen Seele</u>. Studien zu einer Lehre von letzten Haltungen, Bd. 1: Der deutsche Idealismus, Salzburg, A. Pustet, second edition, <u>Prometheus</u>, Studien zur Geschichte des deutschen Idealismus, Heidelberg, F.H. Kerle 1947

1939
A2   <u>Apokalypse der deutschen Seele</u>, Bd. 2: <u>Im Zeichen Nietzsches</u>, Salzburg A. Pustet
A3   Bd. 3: <u>Die Vergöttlichung des Todes</u>, ibid.

1941
A4   <u>Kosmische Liturgie</u>, Höhe und Krise des griechischen Weltbilds bei Maximus Confessor, Freiburg, Herder
French: <u>Liturgie Cosmique</u>, Paris, Aubier 1947
A5   <u>Die Gnostischen Centurien des Maximus Confessor</u>, Herders Theol. Stud. 61

1942
A6   <u>Présence et Pensée</u>. Essai sur la Philosophie Religieuse de Grégoire de Nysse, Paris, Beauchesne

1944
A7   <u>Das christliche Jahr</u>. Text zu Bildern von Richard Seewald, Luzern, Josef Stocker
A8   <u>Das Weizenkorn</u>. Aphorismen, Luzern, Raeber, second edition, Einsiedeln, Johannes-Verlag 1953
A9   <u>Das Herz der Welt</u>, Zuerich, Arche, third edition 1959
Dutch: <u>Het Hart der Wereld</u>, Nijmegen/Antwerpen, Uitgeverij de Koepel 1953
French: <u>Coeur du Monde</u>, Paris, Desclée de Brouwer 1965
Portogese: <u>O Coraçao do Mondo</u>, Porto, Livraria Tavares Martins 1959
Italian: <u>Il Cuore del Mondo</u>, Brescia, Morcelliana 1964
Spanish: <u>El Cor del Mon</u>, Barcelona, Editions 62, 1965
Catalanian: <u>El Corazon del Mondo</u>, Barcelona, Peninsula 1968

1947
A10   <u>Wahrheit</u>. Bd. 1: <u>Wahrheit der Welt</u>, Einsiedeln, Benzinger
French: <u>Phénoménologie de la vérité. La vérité du monde</u>, Paris, Beauchesne 1952
Spanish: <u>La esencia de la verdad</u>, Buenos Aires, Editorial Sudamericana 1955

1948
A11   <u>Der Laie und der Ordensstand</u>, Einsiedeln, Johannes-Verlag, second edition

Freiburg im Br. Herder 1949
French: <u>Laicat et plein apostolat</u>, Liège, La Pensée Catholique et Paris,
Office Général du Livre 1949

1950
A12 <u>Therese von Lisieux</u>. Geschichte einer Sendung, Koeln/Olten, Hegner-
Buecherei, second edition, <u>Schwestern im Geist</u>, Einsiedeln, Johannes-
Verlag 1973
English: <u>Therese of Lisieux</u>, A Story of a Mission, London, Sheed & Ward
1953, New York, Sheed & Ward 1954
Spanish: <u>Teresa de Lisieux</u>, Historia de una Missiòn, Barcelona, Herder
1957

1951
A14 <u>Karl Barth</u>, Darstellung und Deutung seiner Theologie, Koeln/Olten, Hegner-
Buecherei, 2nd edition with new preface, 1962; assumed by Wissenschaft-
liche Buchgemeinschaft, Darmstadt
English: <u>The Theology of Karl Barth</u>, Holt, Rinehart and Winston 1972
abridged edition, Doubleday 1973
A15 <u>Der Christ und die Angst</u>: Einsiedeln, Johannes-Verlag, fifth edition 1961
French: <u>Le Chrétien et l'Angoisse</u>, Paris Desclée de Brouwer 1954
Italian: <u>Il Cristiano et l'Angoscie</u>, Rome, Edizioni Paoline 1957
Spanish: <u>El Cristiano y la Angustia</u>, Madrid, Guadarrama 1960
Portugese: <u>O Cristao e a Angustia</u>, Lisbon, Livraria Morais 1963

1952
A16 <u>Elisabeth von Dijon und ihre geistliche Sendung</u>, Koeln/Olten, Hegner-
Buecherei, second edition <u>Schwestern im Geist</u>, Einsiedeln, Johannes-
Verlag 1973
English: <u>Elizabeth of Dijon</u>, London Harvill Press 1956
French: <u>Elisabeth de la Trinité</u>, Paris, Editions du Seuil 1959
Italian: <u>Suor Elisabetta della Trinità</u>, Milan, Editrice Ancora 1959
A17 <u>Schleifung der Bastionen</u>, Von der Kirche in dieser Zeit, Einsiedeln,
Johannes-Verlag
French: abbreviated in <u>Dieu vivant</u>, 25, 1953, 17-32
Italian: <u>Abbatere i bastioni</u>, Turin, Borla Editore 1966

1953
A18 <u>Reinhold Schneider, sein Weg und sein Werk</u>, Koeln/Olten, Hegner-Buecherei

1954
A19 <u>Thomas von Aquin, Besondere Gnadengaben und die zwei Wege menschlichen
Lebens</u>, Kommentar zu Summa Theologica I-II, 171-182: Deutsche Thomas
Ausgabe Vol 23, Heidelberg und Graz-Wien-Salzburg, Gemeinschaftsverlag
F.H. Kerle: A. Pustet
A20 <u>Bernanos</u>, Koeln/Olten, Hegner-Buecherei, second edition, <u>Gelebte Kirche</u>,
<u>Bernanos</u>, Einsiedeln, Johannes-Verlag 1971
French: <u>Le Chrétien Bernanos</u>, Paris Editions du Seuil 1956

1955
A21 Das betrachtende Gebet: Einsiedeln, Johannes-Verlag
   Italian: La Meditazione, Alba (Cuneo), Edizioni Paoline 1958
   French: La Prière Contemplative, Paris, Desclée de Brouwer 1959
   English: Prayer, London, Geoffrey Chapman 1961, New York, Sheed &
   Ward 1961
   Catalanian: La Pregaria Contemplativa, Barcelona, Editorial Estela 1962
   Dutch: Het Beschouwende Gebed, Hilversum, Paul Brand 1962
   Spanish: La Oración contemplativa, Madrid, Guadarrama 1965
A22 Thessalonicher- und Pastoralbriefe für das betrachtende Gebet erschlossen,
   Einsiedeln, Johannes-Verlag
A23 König David. Text zu den Bildern von Hans Fronius, Einsiedeln, Johannes-
   Verlag

1956
A24 Die Gottesfrage des heutigen Menschen. Wien, Herold
   Flemish: De Moderne Mens op Zoek naar God, Brügge, Desclée de Brouwer
   1957
   French: Dieu et l'Homme d'Aujourd'hui, Paris, Desclée de Brouwer 1958
   English: Science, Religion and Christianity, London, Burns & Oates 1958,
   second edition, The God Question and Modern Man, New York, Seabury 1967
   Spanish: El Problem de Dios en el Hombre Actual, Madrid, Guadarrama
   1960
   Italian: Excerpts: Il Sacramento del fratello, in: Monastica, Monastero di
   S. Scoalstica, Roma 1961, No. 2, 2-8

1957
A25 Parole et Mystère chez Origène, Paris, Editions du Cerf

1958
A26 Einsame Zwiesprache. Martin Buber und das Christentum, Koeln/Olten,
   Hegner
   English: Martin Buber and Christianity, London, Harvill Press 1961.

1959
A27 Theologie der Geschichte. Einsiedeln, Johannes-Verlag
   Spanish: Teologia de la Historia, Madrid, Guadarrama 1959
   French: La Théologie de l'Histoire, Paris, Plon 1960
   English: A Theology of History, New York, Sheed & Ward 1963, London,
   Sheed & Ward 1963
   Italian: Teologia della Storia, Brescia, Morcelliana 1964

1960
A28 Verbum Caro. Skizzen zur Theologie I, Einsiedeln, Johannes-Verlag
   English: Essays in Theology I, Word and Revelation, New York, Herder
   and Herder, 1964
      Essays in Theology II, Word and Redemption, New York, Herder
   and Herder, 1965
   Spanish: Estudios Teológicos, Vol. I, Verbum Caro, Madrid, Guadarrama
   1965

1960
A29   Sponsa Verbi, Skizzen zur Theologie II, Einsiedeln, Johannes-Verlag
English: Church and World, Montreal, Palm Publishers 1967
Italian: Sponsa Verbi, Saggi Theologici II, Brescia, Morcelliana 1969

1961
A30   Herrlichkeit. Eine theologische Aesthetik. vol 1: Schau der Gestalt
Einsiedeln, Johannes-Verlag
French: La Gloire et la Croix, Paris, Aubier 1965
A31   Kosmische Liturgie. Das Weltbild Maximus des Bekenners, Einsiedeln,
Johannes-Verlag; fully revised second edition of A4 and A5

1962
A32   Herrlichkeit. Eine theologische Aesthetik, Bd. 2: Fächer der Stile, Einsiedeln, Johannes-Verlag
French: La Gloire et la Croix, les Aspects Esthétiques de la Révélation,
(2) Styles, 1e partie, D'Irénée à Dante, Paris, Aubier 1968

1963
A33   Das Ganze im Fragment. Aspekte der Geschichtstheologie, Einsiedeln,
Benzinger
English: Theological Anthropology, New York, Sheed & Ward 1967
               Man in History: A Theological Study, London Sheed & Ward 1968
Italian: Il Tutto nel Fragmento, Milano, Jakabook 1970
French: De l'Intégration, Aspects d'une Théologie d'Histoire, Paris,
Desclée de Brouwer 1970
A34   Glaubhaft ist nur Liebe, Einsiedeln, Johannes-Verlag
Dutch: Geloofwaardig is Alleen de Liefde, Hilversum/Antwerpen, Paul
Brand 1963
French: L'Amour Seul est Digne de Foi, Paris, Montaigne 1966
Italian: Solo Amore e Credibile, Torino, Borla Editore 1965
English: Love Alone, New York, Herder and Herder 1969; London, Burns
and Oates 1967
Spanish: Solo el Amor es Digno de Fe, Madrid, Guadarrama 1971

1964
A35   Der Kreuzweg der St. Hedwigs-Kathedrale in Berlin, Mainz, Matthias-
Gruenewald-Verlag
English: The Way of the Cross, London, Burns and Oates 1969

1965
A36   Herrlichkeit. Eine theologische Aesthetik, Bd. 3/1: Im Raum der Meta-
physik, Einsiedeln, Johannes-Verlag
A37   Wer ist ein Christ? Einsiedeln, Benzinger
Spanish: Quién es un Cristiano? Madrid, Guadarrama
French: Qui est un Chrétien? Paris, Coterman; Mulhouse, Salvatore 1966
Italian: Chi e il Cristiano? Queriniana 1969
English: Who is a Christian? Paramus, Paulist/Newman 1968
A38   Wer ist die Kirche? Freiburg i. Br. Herder and Herder

1966

A39   Cordula oder der Ernstfall, Einsiedeln, Johannes-Verlag
English: The Moment of Christian Witness, Westminster, Newman 1969
French: Cordula ou l'Epreuve Décisive, Paris, Beauchesne, 1968
Italian: Cordula, Queriniana 1969
Spanish: Seriedad con las Cosas, 1968

1967

A40   Spiritus Creator, Skizzen zur Theologie III, Einsiedeln, Johannes-Verlag
A41   Herrlichkeit. Eine theologische Aesthetik, Bd. 3/2: Der alte Bund, Einsiedeln, Johannes-Verlag

1968

A42   Erster Blick auf Adrienne von Speyr, Einsiedeln, Johannes-Verlag
A43   Glaube und Naherwartung, Einsiedeln, Benzinger-Verlag, no date
Italian: Anzitutto il Regno di Dio, Moretto 1969
A44   Rechenschaft, 1965; Berthe Widmer, Balthasar-Bibliographie 1965, Einsiedeln, Johannes-Verlag, no date

1969

A45   Theologie der drei Tage, Einsiedeln, Benzinger-Verlag (included in Mysterium Salutis, Bd. 3/2 pp. 137-326, Einsiedeln, Benzinger 1969)
A46   Herrlichkeit, eine theologische Aesthetik, Bd. 3/3: Der neue Bund, Einsiedeln, Johannes-Verlag
A47   Einfaltungen, Muenchen, Koesel Verlag
French: Retour au Centre, 1971
Italian: Con Occhi Semplici, Brescia 1970

1970

A48   Romano Guardini, Reform aus dem Ursprung, Muenchen, Koesel Verlag
French: Romano Guardini, 1971

1971

A49   Klarstellungen, Freiburg im Breisgau, Herder and Herder
French: Point de Repère, 1973
A50   In Gottes Einsatz leben, Einsiedeln, Johannes-Verlag
A51   2 Plädoyers: Balthasar, Warum ich noch ein Christ bin;
                     J. Ratzinger, Warum ich noch in der Kirche bin,
Muenchen, Koesel Verlag
English: Two Say Why, Franciscan Herald, 1973

1972

A52   Die Wahrheit ist symphonisch, Einsiedeln, Johannes-Verlag

1973

A53   Theodramatik, Bd. 1, Prologomena, Einsiedeln, Johannes-Verlag

1974

A54   Pneuma und Institution, Skizzen zur Theologie IV, Einsiedeln, Johannes-Verlag

| B | ESSAYS (selected) |

1938

B8   Philosophie und Theologie des Lebens, in: Das Problem des Lebens in der Forschung: Schriften der Schweizerischen Hochschulzeitung (Zuerich) 1, 46-52

B9   Verstehen oder gehorchen, in: Stimmen der Zeit 69 (Bd. 135), 73-85

1939

B18   Patristik, Scholastik und Wir, in: Theologie der Zeit 3, 65-104

1947

B48   Ueber Sinn und Grenzen christlicher Kontroverse, in: Gloria Dei 1, 205-218

1948

B54   Psychologie der Heiligen? in: Schweizer Rundschau 48, 3-11

1949

B58   Christlicher Humanismus, in: Gloria Dei 4, 37-48

1952

B66   Persönlichkeit und Form, in: Gloria Dei 7, 1-15

1953

B69   Der Begriff der Natur in der Theologie, in: Zeitschrift für katholische Theologie 75, 452-461

B73   Thomas von Aquin im kirchlichen Denken von heute, in: Gloria Dei 8, 65-76

B74   Grösse und Grenze des Amtes, in: Schweizer Rundschau 52, 617-622

B76   Die Stellung von George Bernanos zur Kirche, in: Schweizer Rundschau 53, 253-305

1955

B86   Kleiner Lageplan zu meinen Büchern, in: Schweizer Rundschau 55, 212-225 and Einsiedeln, Johannes-Verlag

1956

B93   Der Tod im heutigen Denken, in: Anima 11, 292-299

1957

B102   Religion et Culture Chrétienne dans le Monde Actuel, in: Comprendre (Venise) 17/18, 1-12

1963

B130   Il Potere dell'Uomo Secondo la Rivelazione Biblica, in: Humanitas (Brescia) 18, 5-15, 113-122

B132   Die Spiritualität Teilhards de Chardin, in: Wort und Wahrheit 18, 339-350

1968

B153, 5 Einigung in Christus, Gedanken über die Vielfalt der biblischen Theologien und der Geist der Einheit im neuen Testament, in: Freiburger Zeitschrift für Philosophie und Theologie 15, 171-189 and in A47

B154   Die Freude und das Kreuz, in: Concilium 4, 683ff

B156   Einheit der theologischen Wissenschaften, in: Hochland 60, 693-703 and
         in A47

1969
B157   Kirche zwischen Links und Rechts, in: Civitas, Maerz, 449-464
B159   Christologie und kirchlicher Gehorsam, in: Geist und Leben 42, 185-203

1970
B160   Christus Gestalt unseres Lebens, zur theologischen Deutung der Eucharistie,
         in: Geist und Leben 43, 173-180

1972
B161   Die drei Gestalten der heutigen Hoffnung, in: Theologische Quartalschrift,
         152, 101-111

C   CONTRIBUTIONS TO COLLECTIONS (selected)

1945
C4   Ueber ein Gedicht von Eichendorf, in: Freundesgabe für Eduard Korrodi,
         Zuerich, Fretz & Wasmuth und Eugen Rentsch Verlag, 133-147

1960
C16   Freiheit, in Freiheit, 6 Radiovorträge, Polis 7, edited by M. Geiger,
         H. Ott, L. Vischer, Zuerich, Evangelischer Verlag, 39-48

1964
C25   Christ und offene Vernunft, in: Die Sorge der Philosophie um den Menschen.
         Helmut Kuhn zum 65. Geburtstag, edited by Franz Widman, Muenchen,
         A. Pustet, 183-191, and in Giornale die Metafisica 6, 553-560

D   TRANSLATIONS (selected)

1938
D2   Origines, Geist und Feuer. Ein Aufbau aus seinen Werken, with an intro-
         duction, 11-41, Salzburg, Otto Mueller; second improved and enlarged
         edition in 1952

F   PREFACES AND POSTSCRIPTS (selected)

F58   Erich Przywara. Sein Schriftum, collected by Leo Zimny, Einsiedeln,
         Johannes-Verlag, 5-18

G   REVIEWS (selected)

1951
G12   Reinhold Schneider, Der grosse Verzicht, Wiesbaden 1950, in: Schweizer
         Rundschau, 51, 505-508

II   OTHER WORKS CITED

BARTH, Karl,   Kirchliche Dogmatik, Zuerich 1932ff

BULTMANN, Rudolf,   Glauben und Verstehen I-IV, Tuebingen 1933ff
History and Eschatology, New York 1962
Jesus Christ and Mythology, New York 1962
Theology of the New Testament, London 1952
"Neues Testament und Mythologie. Das
Problem der Entmythologisierung der neu-
testamentlichen Verkündigung," in Bartsch,
Hans Werner, Kerygma und Mythos I,
Hamburg-Volksdorf, 1948
Entmythologisierung, zusammen mit Schnie-
wind und Barth, Stuttgart 1949

CONGAR, Yves,   "Theologie" in Le Dictionnaire de la Theologie Catholique, vol. 15, Paris

EBELING, Gerhard,   Luther, Einführung in Sein Denken,
Tuebingen, 1964
English: Luther, An Introduction to his
Thought, Philadelphia-Fortress Press 1970
Vom Gebet, Tuebingen, 1963
Das Wesen des Glaubens, Tuebingen 1959
English: The Nature of Faith, Philadelphia-
Fortress Press, 1961
Wort und Glaube I, II, Tuebingen-Mohr,
1965, 1969
English: Word and Faith, Fortress, 1963
Gott und Wort, Tuebingen-Mohr, 1966
English: God and Word, Philadelphia-
Fortress Press, 1967
"Cognitio Dei et hominis," in Geist und Ge-
schichte der Reformation, Festschrift für
Ruechert, Annalen der Kirchengeschichte
38, 1966, pp. 271-322
"Hauptprobleme der protestantischen Theo-
logie der Gegenwart" in Zeitschrift für
Theologie und Kirche (ZThK) 58 1961, 123-
136
"Das Problem des Natürlichen bei Luther,"
in Kirche, Mystik, Heilung und das Natür-
liche bei Luther, Goettingen, 1967, 169-179
"Das Verständnis vom Heil in säkularisierter
Zeit" in Kontexte IV, hg. v. H.J. Schultz,
1967, 5-14
"Der Theologe und Sein Amt," in ZThK 1969,
66ff

"Die Frage nach den Früchten des Geistes,"
in ZThK 1969
"Erwägungen zu einer evangelischen Fundamentaltheologie," in ZThK 67 1970, 479-524
Einführung in Theologische Sprachlehre,
Tuebingen-Mohr, 1971

FUCHS, Ernst,
Marburger Hermeneutik, Tuebingen-Mohr 1968
Glaube und Erfahrung. Gesammelte Aufsätze III,
Tuebingen-Mohr, 1965

GADAMER, Hans,
Wahrheit und Methode, Tuebingen-Mohr, 1960

KAESEMANN, Ernst,
Exegetische Versuche und Besinnungen I, II
Tuebingen-Mohr 1960, 1964
Paulinische Perspektive, Tuebingen-Mohr, 1969
"Zum Thema der urchristlichen Apokalyptik,"
ZThK 59, 1962

deLUBAC, Henri,
"Temoins du Christ," in Civitas, 1965, p. 587-600

NEUMANN, Eric,
"Mystical Man" in The Mystic Vision, Papers
from Eranos Yearbook 6, New York and London
1969
The Origin and History of Consciousness,
Princeton, Princeton University Press 1954
Depth Psychology and a New Ethic, New York
Harper & Row, 1973

PESCH, Otto,
"Existentielle und sapientielle Theologie," in
Theologische Literaturzeitung 92, 1967

RAHNER, Karl,
Schriften zur Theologie IV, VIII, Einsiedeln,
Benzinger-Verlag, 1962
Offenbarung und Ueberlieferung, zusammen mit
Josef Ratzinger, Freiburg im Breisgau, 1965
"Hans Urs von Balthasar," in Civitas, 1965, p.
601-604

ROBINSON, James M.,
Die Neue Hermeneutik, Zuerich, 1965

SCHAEFER, Rolf,
"Gott und Gebet," ZThK 65, 1968

SCHILLEBEECKX, Eduard,
Offenbarung und Theologie, Mainz 1966

SCHWEIZER, Eduard,
"Frage nach dem historischen Jesus," in
Evangelische Theologie 1964

SIEWERTH, Gustav,
Das Schicksal der Metaphysik von Thomas bis
Heidegger, Einsiedeln, Johannes 1959

WRIGHT, G. Ernest,
God Who Acts: Biblical Theology as Recital,
London-SCM Press, Third Edition 1958

12